A *Fresh Look* at
the Mass

A helpful guide to better understand and celebrate the mystery

DAVID M. KNIGHT

**TWENTY-THIRD
PUBLICATIONS**
twentythirdpublications.com

TWENTY-THIRD PUBLICATIONS
One Montauk Avenue, Suite 200, New London, CT 06320
(860) 437-3012 » (800) 321-0411 » www.twentythirdpublications.com

Cover photo: "Seattle St. D's exonarthex window 1-transformed"
by Joe Mabel is licensed under CC BY 2.0

ISBN: 978-1-62785-080-3
Library of Congress Catalog Card Number: 2014959040
Printed in the U.S.A.

A division of Bayard, Inc.

TABLE OF CONTENTS

Take a Fresh Look...

I n over fifty years of presiding at Mass, I have come a long way. But I never realized my true role as priest until 2014, in the mud-hut village of Bongor, in Sierra Leone, Africa.

When we drove up in the parish pickup truck—an old Toyota that had not self-started in seven years—half the village was gathered in the dirt road in front of a mud-bricked, straw-roofed church, singing and dancing. They wore native dress and held wooden tom-toms, tambourines, and castanets.

A cantor was chanting over and over: "Gather, gather, People of God." And as all answered, "Let us give praise and thanksgiving!" the people gathered, coming from all sides of the village. It was the first time I had ever experienced the "gathering song" as what it is named for.

When all were assembled, all dancing, all singing, the cantor changed the words of his chant to "We are the church; holy church-members, enter the church!" And they did, singing and dancing into the little church, building to the rhythm of the tom-toms and the shaking of the tambourines.

And I? I joined the procession, dancing at the end of the line. It was the first time I had ever been the priest at a Mass that began with a whole community entering the church together to celebrate, and myself just one of the crowd.

Now...compare that with how you walk into church on Sunday. What are you feeling? What are you expecting? If you have kids, especially teenagers, what are they expecting? How do they feel about being there? Are they looking forward to celebrating? Or just resigned to enduring?

In our country, the congregation usually sits passively in church, backs to the door, waiting for the presiding priest to start down the aisle. Nothing happens until he does. His entrance begins the celebration. He is the principal figure. The message, unspoken but unconsciously taken for granted by most of the people there, is that the priest is the *only* one who counts. The Mass is something the priest does. What everybody else does is inessential. And many barely participate. They are "there." In the old days, that's all that was required, expected, or even allowed to the laity. That is our cultural heritage.

The truth is, the Mass is something Jesus does, and we are all there to do it with him. This is not clear to everyone yet.

But a new world is opening before us. The Jesuit poet Gerard Manley Hopkins wrote:

> And though the last lights off the black West went
> Oh, morning, at the brown brink eastward springs —
> Because the Holy Ghost over the bent
> World broods with warm breast and with ah! bright wings.

The Mass is being renewed. And the Mass is renewing us— wherever we are willing to let it.

So let's take a deep breath, open our eyes, and take a fresh look at the Mass.

WHAT JESUS COUNTED ON

Imagine you are Jesus at the Last Supper. You are about to die. What will keep your followers together when you are gone? What will keep your words alive among them? What will keep their hearts on fire?

The Holy Spirit. Yes, but not blowing in a vacuum. Your followers are used to God being present among them as a human being, speaking words they can hear, doing things they can see. While you were with them, you kept them together. What will keep them together when you are gone?

The Mass. The celebration of Eucharist. That is the one and only thing. At the Last Supper, Jesus took a loaf of bread, gave thanks (the Greek word from which "Eucharist" comes means to give thanks), broke it, and gave it to his disciples, saying, "This is my body, which is given for you. Do this in remembrance of me" (Luke 22:19). This is a *sacramental* remembrance: a remembrance that *makes present* what we remember.

In the Mass, Jesus is present and acting. That is where we encounter him—not alone, but in company with others: in a communal meal where we listen to his words together, respond to them together, and together experience his presence among us and within each one of us. The Mass holds together all who believe in him, to keep us instructed and our hearts aflame.

Pope Francis wrote: "The joy of the gospel fills the hearts and lives of all who encounter Jesus...I invite all Christians, everywhere, at this very moment, to a renewed personal encounter with Jesus Christ, or at least an openness to letting him encounter them; I ask all of you to do this unfailingly each day" (*The Joy of the Gospel*, nos. 1, 3). The Mass is a way to do that every Sunday. All we have to do is *pay attention* while at Mass, understand what we are paying attention to, and enter into it.

The understanding part is what this book has to offer. When you finish it, I hope you will be thinking more deeply about what you are hearing and seeing at Mass. Then you will be more free to enter into it. If you do, you will experience Mass, not just attend it.

Gradually, your whole life will change.

A FRESH EXPECTATION

In the "old days" (meaning before the Second Vatican Council [1962-1965]), Catholics were taught that it was their obligation to "attend" Mass, just to be there. The focus was on time and space, not on the critical element of participation. A fresh look at the Mass will have us walking through the door prepared to celebrate, prepared to be caught up in the mystery of God, to experience interaction with God himself—Father, Son, and Spirit. We will be ready to praise and thank God. We will become more aware of the gift our life is when enhanced by "the grace of our Lord Jesus Christ."

Walking into church will be like leaving Kansas for Oz—except that the "Oz" we are immersed in during Mass is the real world, and the "Kansas" of our cultural environment outside of Mass is largely make-believe. We will enter into Mass to be at home.

MYSTERY IS OUR HOME

Eucharist takes us—and also the world we live in, if we bring it to Mass with us—into the reality of *mystery*. Eucharist makes present to us what always was, is now, and always will be. Eucharist surrounds us with the pervading presence of infinite Being, infinite Truth and Love. Eucharist catches us up in the action of God that explains all actions and gives them their true value. Eucharist, if we know how to enter into it, makes us real.

We need to take a fresh look at Eucharist and see how it does this—to look at the Mass as if we had never seen or heard it before. If we do, we may find ourselves seeing and hearing things we have never seen or heard in our lives. We will come to experience Eucharist as "the source and summit," the starting point and the high point of every week—indeed of our Christian life.

A fresh look at the Mass will give us a new way of seeing ourselves and, because of this, a new way of perceiving our participation in the celebration. We won't be there to "hear" Mass, or even to "follow" the Mass as the priest celebrates it. We will be there to *offer* Mass together with Jesus and others—*with* Christ and *as* Christ—to offer Jesus to the Father for the life of the human race, and to offer ourselves with him and in him: our flesh with his "for the life of the world."

The first sign of this new look will be that we won't wait for the presider to "begin Mass." From the very first moment of the celebration, we will experience ourselves making the Mass happen. We will be doing it—living it, loving it. We will begin by entering into the first hymn, the "gathering song," with enthusiasm, listening to the words of the hymn and drawing upon them to give our excitement focus. Sometimes we might even dance!

From the very first moment of the celebration, we will experience ourselves making the Mass happen.

For prayer and discussion

- What do you think about on your way to Mass?

- How do you feel about going to Mass?

- How would you feel about dancing into church?

- Do you see Mass more as something the priest does or you do?

- What difference would it make in your life if you couldn't get to Mass?

- Do you feel like pursuing this? Do you think it might help you bring others back to Mass?

CHAPTER ONE

"In the name..."
The World of Relationship with God

A fresh look at the Mass literally takes us "out of this world." The very first words the presider speaks lift us up into a new world. We enter the world of *mystery*—the world of conscious relationship with God.

What gives us the right to gather for Mass?

What allows us ordinary people to presume the privilege of an audience with God? Or the right to ask God for anything—especially if we venture to speak for others? Who are we to even lift up our voices to praise God? Are we on a high-enough level to praise the infinite Being of God? God's incomprehensible Goodness, Truth, and Beauty? By what right do we deal with God at all? In whose name, by whose invitation, do we present ourselves at the door?

It is "in the name of the Father!"

We are here because the Father has "held us worthy to be in his presence and minister to him." We are here "in the name of the Father," because we are the family he wants to be here with him.

And we present ourselves "in the name of the Son," our "Lord Jesus Christ, at whose command we celebrate these mysteries." Because he said, "Do this in memory of me."

"And of the Holy Spirit," because we are gathered, not just in the name of obedience to church law, or of our common faith as Catholics, or even in the name of the personal desire each of us has to worship God. We are gathered in the "communion of the Holy Spirit." In everything we say and do, we will be giving expression to the Spirit surging and singing within us. We assemble in the name of the Holy Spirit, who "fills the hearts of his faithful, and enkindles in them the fire of his divine love."

The opening words of the Mass are a propulsion into mystery.

We are gathering "in the name of" the Three Persons of the Holy Trinity! That means we are caught up in the infinite mystery of God. We are entering into conscious relationship with God himself as Father, Son, and Spirit.

And since every relationship is a way of *interacting* with another, the Mass is gathering us together to interact with God the "Father," as infinite Being and Goodness; with God the Son, as "Word" of God, infinite Truth; and with God the "Holy Spirit," as infinite Love.

This catches us up into the mystery of God's divine life—the interaction taking place between the Three Persons of God.

Real world—Unreal world

We may think of the celebration of Eucharist, not as the beginning of our week, but as a "time out," after which we return to the "real" world of family, school and social life, business and politics. Nothing could be more mistaken.

To be "real," the world must have all the authentic dimensions of human life that Saint Paul held up to us: "I pray that you may have the power to comprehend, with all the saints, what is the breadth and length and height and depth, and to know the love of Christ that surpasses knowledge, so that you may be filled with all the fullness of God" (Ephesians 3:18–19).

The problem is, our secular culture frequently blurs these dimensions. The false world of "secular culture" in which we live doesn't acknowledge relationship with God. It doesn't deny it either. It just ignores it, which takes it out of our consciousness more than denial would. Our society doesn't remind us of God, doesn't call us to praise, thank, or worship the Three Persons, doesn't summon us to prayer. Except for the presence of church buildings with their singular architecture, nothing in the city reminds us that God exists.

True, if we "have eyes to see," we can see through all creation to the Creator. We can recognize God's gift and presence in everything around us, and we can praise and thank God. But nothing in the man-made environment we call our "culture" calls us to this. Wordsworth protested poetically against it:

> The world is too much with us; late and soon,
> Getting and spending, we lay waste our powers;
> Little we see in Nature that is ours;
> We have given our hearts away, a sordid boon!
> This Sea that bares her bosom to the moon;
> The winds that will be howling at all hours,
> And are up-gathered now like sleeping flowers;
> For this, for everything, we are out of tune;
> It moves us not....

The world we live and play and work in just passes over in silence what is most deep, most true, most important, most all-present in human life. That world is unreal. So we return again to Mass to renew our contact with reality.

Mass *is* the real world, a world in which everything we hear and see speaks to us about the authentic relationship between God and all creation. The real world reflects the Existence from which all existence comes: the existence of God, who is Existence itself. And God's existence, we know from revelation, is *relationship*: the Three Persons are "one in Being," but differ through their relationship (interaction) with each other. Their identity as Father, Son, and Spirit becomes clear through the different facets of the Godhead each reveals. So all existence that comes from God is characterized by relationship. Our true identity—who we are—is determined by our relationships, by our interaction with other beings and with God himself.

To be aware of ourselves as authentic human beings, we have to interact with God as Creator, through praise and thanksgiving. To know ourselves as children of God by baptism, we have to interact with God as Father. Jesus taught us how to do this (see Matthew, chapters five and six). To enter into personal relationship with Jesus, we have to interact with him as human persons interact with each other. To realize we have received the Holy Spirit, we have to interact with him, asking and listening for his inspirations. By the gift of divine life we are caught up in the knowing, loving interaction of the Three Persons. The real world is a world that acknowledges this.

And to be authentic members of the human race, we have to interact with one another as persons, the way the Father, Son, and Spirit interact with each other: "equal in majesty, undivided in splendor." As persons we all are equal; nothing differentiates us except the way we freely interact with God, each other, and the world.

That is not the world we live in. It is a world we are called to *create*—to fashion out of everything that makes up our daily life. And the Mass is our weekly starting point.

THE "SIGN OF THE CROSS"

When we begin Eucharist "in the name of the Father, and of the Son, and of the Holy Spirit," we enter explicitly into the real world: the world of relationship—of interaction—with God.

The Sign of the Cross is the oldest Christian profession of faith. In the late second century, Tertullian wrote: "In all our travels and movements, when coming in and going out, when putting on our shoes, at the bath, at the table, in lighting our candles, in lying down, in sitting down, whatever we are doing, we mark our foreheads with the sign of the cross."

What are we saying when we do this?

First we lift up our hand—and heart—to heaven, as many do when they pray to God. But the difference is, we put our hand on our *head*, on our forehead, to say we *know* him. He is not "the man upstairs" for us; he is our *Father*. He gives us his own divine life. Then we bring our hand *down* and place it on our heart to say God came down from heaven as Jesus the *Son* to be one of us, to take flesh and live in us as his body on earth. He lives and acts *with us, in us,* and *through us* to continue his mission of giving life to the world. Then we sweep our hand in an arc from one shoulder to the other to say that the *Holy Spirit is* within us, sending us out and empowering us to unite the whole world in one divine family of love.

All of this expresses the meaning, and is the fruit, of the *cross*, on which, by baptism, we died in Christ and rose again with him as a "new creation." If we understand the Sign of the Cross, we understand the mystery of Christianity.

At Mass we begin our week with the Sign of the Cross. It expresses the *identity* we have through relationship with the Three Persons of God. We can use it all week to remind us of who we are. We can "extend the Mass" by making the sign of the cross when we wake up and go to bed, when we sit down to table or get into the car, whenever we turn on a computer or pick up a cell phone.

The Mass reminds us to do everything we do *"in the name"* of the relationship we have with Father, Son, and Spirit. Why not carry that reminder into the world outside? By making the sign of the cross, we can express all week long our awareness of the relationship that people have with each other and with God that we receive at Mass.

For prayer and discussion

- Do you ever feel that you or people around you are living a "low ceiling life"—that is, one that doesn't give a human room to breathe?

- What is the first thing that comes to mind when you think of being a Christian? Is it interacting with the Father, Son, and Spirit in a personal relationship?

- What do you see or hear at work, on the street, in stores, or even at home that reminds you of the *breadth and length and height and depth* of human life as Jesus revealed it? How do you see and hear these dimensions celebrated at Mass?

- What do you do—all day and every day—that reminds you of your relationship with God?

- How often do you make the sign of the cross? Do you think you should make it in public?

- In your opinion, what is the most striking reality expressed in the Mass? Is this passed over in silence in ordinary life? If so, how does that affect daily living?

CHAPTER TWO

"The grace of our Lord Jesus Christ..."

We Are Divine

W̶e begin Mass by declaring who we really are. The presider announces it in the words of his greeting: "The grace of our Lord Jesus Christ, and the love of God [the Father], and the communion of the Holy Spirit be with you all." This tells us who we are in relationship to the Father, Son, and Holy Spirit. That is the key to our existence.

If we listen, the words we hear at Mass will give us a fresh view of life. The Introductory Rites (everything before the readings) are an exciting celebration of who we are.

THE GRACE OF OUR LORD JESUS CHRIST

What is the "grace of our Lord Jesus Christ"?

In one line, "grace" is *the gift of sharing in God's own divine life.* Isn't that an awesome way to see yourself? The reality is, you are divine. Is that the way they see you in the world you live and work in? Is that the way you see yourself? Or do people just take you for an ordinary human being, assuming, when they look at you, that "what you see is what you get"?

Blindness. Illusion. Totally false! Unless people see you, and you see yourself, as sharing in the divine life of God, enlightened by Infinite Truth, empowered by Infinite Love, living the Infinite Life of Father, Son, and Spirit, a member of the immediate family of God, they simply don't know you—and you don't know yourself. The truth is, you are a continuance of the real presence of Jesus Christ in the world. You are his own living body on earth. More, you are divine. In fact, the effect of your baptism was that you "became Christ." These are the words of Saint Augustine, affirmed in the *Catechism of the Catholic Church* (795): "Let us rejoice and give thanks, for we have become not only Christians, but Christ…Marvel and rejoice: *we have become Christ!*"

In the real world of Eucharist, you are recognized as the mystery of a human being sharing in the divine life of God because you accepted to give your body to Jesus at baptism to be his body. You and Jesus share one body. You became what he is: a son or daughter of the Father "in the Son." You live and love and act by his Spirit. And he became what you are: a man or woman, child or adult, doctor, student, salesperson, or mechanic. You are alive both by the human life you received from your parents and by the divine life you receive through union with Jesus Christ, God the Son. That makes God the Father your real Father. You are a real son or daughter of God.

You share in the life of the Trinity. You are part of it, caught up in it. This is not a matter of conscious experience. It is more true, more real, than human experience is. It is something you know by faith, which can be defined as "the gift of sharing in God's own knowing act."

By faith you know what God knows as God knows it. But you cannot translate this knowledge into adequate human thoughts and words. By faith "we see in a mirror, dimly," but when the veil is removed at death "we will see face to face." Then we "will know fully," even as we are already fully known by God (1 Corinthians 13:12; see also 2 Corinthians 3:18).

Eucharist is an anticipation of this. Eucharist translates our faith into words and gestures. In Eucharist, we celebrate the truth that is. We acknowledge it and make ourselves aware of it. The words of the liturgy proclaim it to us. They bring us out of the darkness of human perception that impregnates our culture and into the real world. That is why we need to take a fresh look at Eucharist and see what it really says. We will find ourselves understanding truths we have never understood or appreciated in our lives.

OUR TRUE RELATIONSHIP WITH JESUS

The mystery that the "ordinary" world ignores and Eucharist proclaims is that we are never alone. Jesus is always with us. This calls us into constant *personal relationship* (interaction) with Jesus. That is what Christianity is. Jesus is not just with us like a friend by our side. He is that. But he is also *in* us. This is the mystery of "the grace of our Lord Jesus Christ."

We know that God is in everything he has made, filling all things with existence, power, and beauty. St. Ignatius has us ponder this in the culminating meditation of his *Spiritual Exercises*, entitled "A Contemplation for Obtaining Love":

> I will consider how God *dwells in* creatures; in the elements, giving them existence; in the plants, giving them life; in the animals, giving them sensation; in human beings, giving them intelligence; and finally, how in this way he dwells also in myself, giving me existence, life, sensation and intelli-

gence; and even further, making me his temple, since I am created as a likeness and image of the Divine Majesty.

...I will consider how God *labors and works for me* in all the creatures on the face of the earth....For example, he is working in the heavens, elements, plants, fruits, cattle, and all the rest—giving them their existence, conserving them, concurring with their vegetative and sensitive activities, and so forth.

(*THE SPIRITUAL EXERCISES*, 234, TR. GEORGE GANSS, SJ, LOYOLA UNIVERSITY PRESS, 1992)

God is in all his creatures, empowering them to do what they do. But through grace, God has come into us to do his own "divine thing." And to do it in and through our human activities.

The mystery of "the grace of our Lord Jesus Christ" is that we are in *partnership* with Jesus to live one shared life in one shared body. We "co-act" with Jesus in actions that are both human and divine, actions that are both his and ours. Jesus acts divinely in our human actions, w*ith us, in us,* and *through us.* We act divinely "through him, with him, and in him." We are acting "in Christ" and Christ is acting "in us."

With the words "the grace of our Lord Jesus Christ...be with you," the Eucharist reminds us that we get up every morning to let Jesus do something divine—*with us, in us,* and *through us*—in everything we do that day. This is what Jesus was talking about when he said, "I am the vine, you are the branches. Those who abide *in me* and I *in them* bear much fruit, because apart from me you can do nothing" (John 15:5).

A good way to keep yourself conscious of this is to start saying the "WIT prayer" all day long:

Lord, I give you my body.
Live this day *with* me,
live this day *in* me,
live this day *through* me.

Add, if you want, "Let me think with your thoughts, and speak with your words, and act as your body on earth."

W-ith, I-n, T-hrough: WIT. Say it as soon as you wake up, before you even open your eyes. And keep saying it all day long. All day, before everything you do, keep repeating: "Lord, do this *with* me, do this *in* me, do this *through* me." To say this prayer all day long will make you aware, make you conscious, that by the "grace of our Lord Jesus Christ," you are sharing in the divine life of God. The words of the presider's greeting at Mass are an invitation to cultivate that awareness.

To be aware of who you are through your divine relationship with Jesus Christ is a mystical experience. Take it out with you from Mass and live a life that is real.

For prayer and discussion

- How does it feel to be aware that Jesus is living in your body and acting through you in everything you do?

- Do you intend to start saying the WIT prayer all day? How much trouble would it be to form the habit? What could you use to remind you?

- What other ways can you think of that will keep you conscious all day long of your relationship with Christ?

CHAPTER THREE

"And the love of God..."

The True Image of the Father

The presider's greeting continues: "and the love of God..." In some translations—the French, Spanish, German, Portuguese, Italian, and Polish, for example—this second phrase is: *"and the love of the Father."* This is because the clear intention of the greeting is to proclaim our identity as related to the Three Persons of the Trinity. All who are assembled for Eucharist have received "the grace of our Lord Jesus Christ," the Son. All of us know "the love of the Father." All of us are united in the "communion of the Holy Spirit."

The second phrase of the greeting is inviting us to feel welcome in the house of our Father, to feel at home, safe, protected, loved, and appreciated. The Father's love is embracing us in a communal hug that draws us into the warm family life of God, where all of us are united with the Three Persons and with each another. We are loved. God loved us before we were born, loves us now, and will love us without end. Forever.

This is the Father who gave and is giving us existence:

> You formed my inmost being. You knit me together in my
> mother's womb. I will give thanks to you, for I am fearfully
> and wonderfully made…You saw me before I was born…
> How precious are your thoughts about me, O God! They
> are innumerable! I could never count them!…And when I
> wake up in the morning, you are still with me!
> (PSALM 139:13–18)

He is the Father who unfailingly provides for us:

> Do not worry about your life, what you will eat or what
> you will drink, or about your body, what you will wear…
> Your heavenly Father knows that you need all these things.
> (MATTHEW 6:25, 32)

And, above all, he is the Father who shares with us his own divine life—the greatest intimacy that can exist:

> See what love the Father has given us, that we should be
> called children of God; and that is what we are. (1 JOHN 3:1)

> On that day you will know that I am in my Father, and
> you in me, and I in you…Those who love me will keep my
> word, and my Father will love them, and we will come to
> them and make our home with them. (JOHN 14:20, 23)

The greeting proclaims this, identifying us as people who know "the love of the Father." It invites each one of us to ask if this is true of ourselves. If our experience in Christianity, in the religion we grew up in, was not the experience of relationship with a loving Father, it was not the experience we celebrate in Eucharist. If we do not know, if we have not experienced, the love of the Father, we have never experienced authentic Christianity. We have never really heard the Good News. Then the greeting becomes for us "evangelization"—the proclamation of a gospel we have not yet truly heard.

Even the religion we grew up in may not have been the real world. It may have been a falsified Christianity, a distorted and "unreal" version of the Catholic Church. The bishops who assembled for the Second Vatican Council acknowledged this. They made the shocking declaration that the church itself may have contributed to the "rise of atheism" by teaching Catholic doctrines falsely!

> Atheism is not present in people's minds from the beginning. It springs from various causes, among which must be included a critical reaction against religions, and in some places against the Christian religion in particular. Believers can thus have more than a little to do with the rise of atheism. To the extent that they are careless about their instruction in the faith, or present its teaching falsely, or even fail in their religious, moral, or social life, they must be said to conceal rather than reveal the authentic face of God and religion. (*THE CHURCH IN THE MODERN WORLD,* NO. 19)

We who grew up in the church before the Second Vatican Council often experienced this. The Father of Jesus who was presented to us sometimes came across as a monster. We were taught it was a mortal sin to miss Mass on a single Sunday. This meant that if a nine-year-old girl stayed in bed on a single Sunday morning because she was just too lazy to get up and go to Mass, God would burn that child in the fires of hell for all eternity! There are some still teaching that in the church today.

Our teachers apparently were not aware of what they were saying about God when they said something was a "mortal sin." To identify a particular action as a "mortal sin" is to identify God as a Father who will disown and damn to hell forever any child of his who performs that action.

My own brother grew up so terrified of God that to save his sanity he simply denied God's existence. Today, at age eighty-seven, he is still denying it. This is because the teaching he received in church and in Catholic schools "concealed rather than revealed the authentic face of God and religion."

We did not realize in those days that when we called something a "mortal sin," we might be blaspheming by making "the face of God" the face of a monster.

Woe to those who are doing it today: those who dare to declare lightly that something is a "mortal sin." If they are wrong, they are blaspheming the "love of the Father." They may be guilty of a sin much worse than the one they are defining as "mortal."

Fortunately, the church is always changing, always correcting her mistakes.

Pope Francis recognizes that not everything taught *in* the church is the authentic teaching *of* the church. He warns us that clinging to the outdated words of the past out of a desire for doctrinal security can blind us:

> If the Christian is a restorationist [someone who wants

to "restore" the pre-Vatican II church], or a legalist; if he wants everything clear and safe, then he will find nothing. Tradition and memory of the past must help us to have the courage to open up new areas to God. Those who today always look for solutions through law-enforcement, those who long for an exaggerated doctrinal "security," those who stubbornly try to recover a past that no longer exists—they have a static and inward-directed view of things. In this way, faith becomes an ideology among other ideologies. (SEE HIS AMERICA MAGAZINE INTERVIEW, SEPTEMBER 30, 2013.)

Those, however, who continue to "gather together with the church" for Eucharist are gradually being brought more and more authentically into the real world of Catholic belief and practice—if they listen to the words.

DEFINE EVERY LAW BY LOVE
If God is a God of love, any law that is harsh, unfeeling, or cruel cannot be a law of God. If we look at laws to understand God, instead of looking at God to understand his laws, we will fall into the sin of the Pharisees as they are portrayed in the gospel: "They tie up heavy burdens, hard to bear, and lay them on the shoulders of others; but they themselves are unwilling to lift a finger to move them" (Matthew 23:4). But if we see all laws in the light of God's love, we will understand what our Father meant to say.

Jesus said: "Come to me, all you that are weary and are carrying heavy burdens, and I will give you rest. Take my yoke upon you, and learn from me; for I am gentle and humble in heart, and you will find rest for your souls. For my yoke is easy, and my burden is light" (Matthew 11:28–30).

It is in this spirit that the greeting invites us to enter into Mass.

For prayer and discussion

- What helps you most to feel that God is your loving Father?

- Did the teaching you received in the church (which you may have accepted too trustingly as the teaching *of* the church) make you feel total trust in God as a loving Father?

- Do you know how any of the saints felt about God the Father? For example, St. Thérèse, the "Little Flower"?

CHAPTER FOUR

"And the communion of the Holy Spirit..."

Together on the Level of Mystery

The third thing the presider proclaims in his greeting is that, as Christians, we are united in the "communion of the Holy Spirit." He proclaims this to make sure everyone is conscious of the *mystery* of who we are and of our relationship with each other.

What is the "communion of the Holy Spirit"?

The Eucharist proclaims that the real bond of union between Christians is the mystical experience of being enlightened, inspired, moved, and guided by the indwelling presence of the Holy Spirit in each one's heart, an experience we should all become conscious of in Eucharist.

Yes, a certain agreement about doctrines, rules, and practices is essential to full communion with each other. But there is more real "communion of the Holy Spirit" between those consciously living and interacting with God on the divine level of grace—even if there is some disunion on the level of words and practices—than there is between totally "orthodox" Catholics who don't know what it is to interact personally with God. A religion of law observance, focused on the "right" doctrinal formulations, rules, and practices, is just that: a "religion." It is not a "spirituality," because spirituality requires experience of the spirit: one's own spirit and the Spirit of God. All those who commune in spirit with God can have "communion of the Holy Spirit" with one another. And only those who do are in the "real world" of Christianity. That is where the Eucharist calls us to be. That is the experience that full, conscious, and active participation in the Mass can give us.

A fresh look at the Mass will refresh our view of Christianity. It might also change the way we perceive our relationship with other Christians, both in and outside of the Catholic Church.

For Pope Francis, the starting point of our interaction (relationship) with anybody should be the discovery and mutual acknowledgment of what we have in common—that is, any truth, any goodness, any human value we share, without attaching labels to it, religious or otherwise. Once we "shake hands" in mutual agreement on our common human (or mystical) experience, we can sit down, have a cup of coffee, and begin to sort out our differences. There is no other way to do it as friends.

The name for this is "dialogue"—trying to understand rather than condemn. The starting point and the goal of the process are the same: love that seeks the other's good. But we ought to know the theological basis this love is built on, the doctrine of faith that helps us understand what we are doing. It is the "communion of the Holy Spirit" that we announce at the beginning of Mass. Pope Francis himself explained this in his audience on October 30, 2013:

Today I would like to speak about a very beautiful reality of

our faith, namely, the "communion of saints"...This is one
of the most consoling truths of our faith, since it reminds
us that we are not alone but that there is a communion of
life among all those who belong to Christ...all those who
believe in the Lord Jesus and are incorporated by him into
the Church through Baptism...

By the definition Francis gives, we share "communion of the
Holy Spirit" not only with Catholics and the Orthodox, but with
all who believe in Jesus Christ:

> The Church, in her most profound truth, is communion
> with God, intimacy with God, a communion of love
> with Christ and with the Father in the Holy Spirit, which
> extends to our communion as brothers and sisters. This
> relationship between Jesus and the Father is the "matrix"
> of the bond between us Christians...
>
> How beautiful it is to support each other in the wonder-
> ful adventure of faith!...In this communion—communion
> means "common-union"—we form a great family, where
> every member is helped and sustained by the others.

Unfortunately, instead of recognizing our "communion of the
Holy Spirit," we often close ourselves up in "sociological" defi-
nitions that divide us from one another according to doctrinal
differences. We deny sacramental Communion to one another
because we are not in "full communion" on the formulation of
doctrine. We ignore the mystery of the divine light of faith given
to all in baptism that unites us more deeply on the level of the
revealed, inexpressible truth of God than its translation into the
human words of doctrinal formulations ever could.

Eucharist is meant to be a source of unity, not an experience of division. This is what we affirm in every Mass when the presider says to everyone present: "the communion of the Holy Spirit be with you all."

This communion is not perfect. It was not perfect in the early church, and it is not perfect now, even among Catholics who are all in "good standing." The Council bishops acknowledged that "even in the beginnings of this one and only church of God there arose certain rifts (see 1 Corinthians 1:10–13; 11:18–22; Galatians 1:6–9; 1 John 2:18–19), which the Apostle Paul strongly condemned." In different degrees, Catholics have continued to fight each other from the first days of the early church when there was division between Peter and Paul:

> When Cephas [Peter] came to Antioch, I [Paul] opposed him to his face, because he stood self-condemned. For until certain people came from James, he used to eat with the Gentiles. But after they came, he drew back and kept himself separate for fear of the circumcision faction. And the other Jews joined him in this hypocrisy, so that even Barnabas was led astray by their hypocrisy. But when I saw that they were not acting consistently with the truth of the gospel, I said to Cephas before them all, "If you, though a Jew, live like a Gentile and not like a Jew, how can you compel the Gentiles to live like Jews?" We ourselves are Jews by birth and not Gentile sinners; yet we know that a person is justified not by the works of the law but through faith in Jesus Christ. And we have come to believe in Christ Jesus, so that we might be justified by faith in Christ, and not by doing the works of the law, because no one will be justified by the works of the law. (GALATIANS 2:11–16)

That means we cannot judge people's internal adherence to Jesus by their external observance of rules. We have to look deeper than that.

Peter and Paul resolved their differences, and both died as martyrs in Rome, united in common testimony to one faith. That is why whoever is bishop of Rome inherits the role of both Peter and Paul, charged with keeping the church faithful to tradition while responsive to the Spirit of change. This includes working for "communion" with non-Catholics. As Pope Francis said on the feast of the Conversion of Saint Paul, 2014: "Today the Petrine ministry cannot be fully understood without openness to dialogue with all believers in Christ."

But all Catholics did not succeed in resolving their differences as Peter and Paul did. The Council bishops continue the story:

> But in subsequent centuries much more serious dissensions made their appearance and quite large communities came to be separated from full communion with the Catholic Church—for which, often enough, people of both sides were to blame. The children who are born into these Communities and who grow up believing in Christ cannot be accused of the sin involved in the separation, and *the Catholic Church embraces them as brothers and sisters,* with respect and affection. For *people who believe in Christ and have been truly baptized are in communion with the Catholic Church even though this communion is imperfect.* The differences that exist in varying degrees between them and the Catholic Church—whether in doctrine and sometimes in discipline, or concerning the structure of the Church—do indeed create many obstacles, sometimes serious ones, to full ecclesiastical communion. The ecu-

menical movement is striving to overcome these obstacles. But even in spite of them it remains true that *all who have been justified by faith in Baptism are members of Christ's body, and have a right to be called Christian, and so are correctly accepted as brothers and sisters by the children of the Catholic Church.* (DECREE ON ECUMENISM, 3; ITALICS ADDED)

This is what we are announcing when we proclaim our "communion of the Holy Spirit" at the beginning of Mass.

It is explicit Catholic teaching (see the *Catechism of the Catholic Church*, nos. 1258-1260) that we can also share this deep unity with non-Christians who, without knowing it, have accepted the "grace of our Lord Jesus Christ" under some other name.

We must not forget that, for Catholics, in addition to sacramental baptism with water, there is also "baptism of desire." This is the way God redeems, through union with Christ, people who have never heard of Jesus, or who cannot accept him because of their negative experience of Christianity—like Mahatma Gandhi. He said, "I like your Christ, I do not like your Christians. Your Christians are so unlike your Christ." God sends them, as he sent the Magi, a "star"—a symbol they can relate to—inviting total, unconditional surrender to the unspecified Truth and Goodness it calls them to. If they accept, they are what theologian Karl Rahner called "anonymous Christians."

To understand what Catholics mean by the expression "baptism of desire," read Matthew 2:1–12 and ask yourself, "If those 'pagan' star-gazers had died in the desert on the way to Bethlehem, following their star, would they have died Christians?" Catholics believe that all who, with unconditional faith, "follow the star" that God has sent them, believing in whatever it is leading them to, are already "anonymous Christians." We know, even if they don't, that their star is leading to Jesus.

A fresh look at the Mass summons us to look for "communion of the Holy Spirit" wherever and in whomsoever it might exist.

For prayer and discussion

• When do you most feel "communion of the Holy Spirit" with another person or group?

• Do you feel more religious rapport with some Protestants than you do with some Catholics? If so, why?

• How many people have you talked to, Catholic or not, about their *experience* of God? Did it give you a sense of communion with them?

• Do you think Mahatma Gandhi was a Christian without knowing it? (If you don't know much about Gandhi, take the Dalai Lama or some other non-Christian the world respects.)

CHAPTER FIVE

The Penitential Act

The Equality of Sinners

After the greeting, the presider continues: "Brothers and sisters, let us acknowledge our sins, and so prepare ourselves to celebrate the sacred mysteries." This is the "great equalizing" at the start of Mass. Frequently, the prayer that follows says:

I confess to Almighty God,
and to you, my brothers and sisters,
that I have greatly sinned…

At Mass, the pope introduces himself as a sinner. So do bishops, priests, nuns, alcoholics, corporate executives, prison inmates, and presidents of nations, if they are Catholic. Once we have recognized in the greeting our divine dignity and relationship with God and each other "in Christ," we go on to present ourselves only as "sinners." We claim no other titles or dignities. We stand on the common ground of our shared sinfulness, discounting everything else. No one is "higher" or "lower," more holy or more heinous than anyone else. There is no one present who doesn't deserve to be there, because the only requirement for admission is the admission that none of us deserves to be there. Everyone is equally undeserving and equally accepted.

We all begin Mass as equals. Acceptance into the Christian community does not depend on good behavior. Only those who refuse to admit they are sinners like everyone else are "not acceptable."

Webster's Dictionary defines sin as "the breaking of religious law or of a moral principle." It makes no reference to any personal relationship. The *Catechism of the Catholic Church* defines sin better as "a failure in genuine love for God" or as "an offense against God" (nos. 1849, 1850). The Eucharist, however, focuses on sin as a reality common to us all—and then it makes positive use of our sinfulness to unite us to each other in mutual equality and acceptance. We begin Mass identifying ourselves as sinners: "I confess to almighty God, and to you, my brothers and sisters, that I have greatly sinned…" This, with baptism, is the "membership card" that admits us to Eucharist. We are all sinners. We are all the same. No one is claiming to be better than anyone else.

God forgives and accepts us all. The price of entry into the eucharistic celebration is that we must forgive and accept everyone as God does, and pray for each other with hope. We have confidence that all the "angels and saints" in heaven accept us, as do all our "brothers and sisters" on earth. And so each of us asks everyone else with confidence to "pray for me to the Lord our God."

This is the real world.

Out there in the phony world of protocol and social conventions we suffer the unreal evaluation of people embodied in the honors, prestige, and established "pecking order" of society. It is all a lie. The famous poet Rudyard Kipling recognized this with class-conscious cynicism in his poem "The Ladies," which concludes, "For the Colonel's Lady and Judy O'Grady / Are sisters under their skins!" That might have been a shocking line in the unreal world of Victorian England. But in the real world of Eucharist, it is a self-evident starting point.

In his more solemn poem "Recessional," Kipling deflated the prideful pretensions of nations:

> Far-called, our navies melt away;
> On dune and headland sinks the fire:
> Lo, all our pomp of yesterday
>   Is one with Nineveh and Tyre!...
> The tumult and the shouting dies;
>   The Captains and the Kings depart:
> Still stands Thine ancient sacrifice,
>   An humble and a contrite heart.
> Lord God of Hosts, be with us yet,
> *Lest we forget—lest we forget!*

Eucharist keeps us from forgetting. It reminds us of what we are—and what we are not. No one should feel uncomfortable or feel judged coming to Mass. Down deep, we all see ourselves as being just as sinful as everybody else. We may not "commit sins" as obviously as some others do, but if we know our hearts, our spontaneous prayer is, "Lord, have mercy on me, a sinner."

Then we know we belong. The Pharisees "grumbled" and said about Jesus, "This fellow welcomes sinners and eats with them" (Luke 15:2). He still does. They are the ones the Mass is for. If we join them, we will find ourselves with Jesus.

The "Penitential Rite" is our rite—and right—of admission.

For prayer and discussion

- Does it make you feel good to belong to a church where everyone is a sinner and knows it?

- When you say at Mass, "I confess...that I have sinned," do you feel united with everyone else? Accepted and accepting?

- Do you ever feel that you shouldn't be at Mass? Has this chapter removed those doubts?

- Do you know any people who don't come to Mass because they don't feel accepted? What can you do about that?

CHAPTER SIX

The "Kyrie"
We Are Family

After our confession of sin, the Eucharist brings us again into the truth of our relationship with God. We ask God for "mercy." It is important to understand this word. It tells us we are all one family with God.

"Have mercy" does not just mean "Help!" "Have mercy" is a translation of the Greek *eleison*. It is rooted in the Semitic word for a mother's womb. It means to come to the aid of another *out of a sense of relationship*. In Spanish it is translated *piedad*, from the Latin *pietas*, which in ancient Rome was the "gut bond" of loyalty to family, hearth, and homeland.

We don't "have mercy" when we give help to others just because they are needy. There can be a whiff of condescension in this. That is what moved St. Vincent de Paul to caution his Sisters of Charity, "Pray that the poor will forgive you the bread you give them!" We "have mercy" only when our help to others is based on the recognition of a bond of relationship like that of family. Then there is no feeling of superiority. When the help we give comes from a sense of identification, of relationship, not condescension, it will be "mercy." And so, when we ask God to "have mercy," we are reminding him and ourselves that by sharing his own divine life with us he has made us family. We are not just his creatures; we are his relatives.

When Jesus taught us in turn to "have mercy" on everyone else in need, he extended "love of neighbor" and the "family bond" of mercy to embrace the whole family of the human race. This is something recognized in the real world of Eucharist but that we cannot take for granted outside. It is not a relationship acknowledged in the restrictive world of exclusive neighborhoods and national boundaries. This is something Pope Francis has frequently reminded us of:

> The Church...is called to be the People of God which embraces all peoples...for the face of each person bears the mark of the face of Christ! Here we find the deepest foundation of the dignity of the human person...It is less the criteria of efficiency, productivity, social class, or ethnic or religious belonging which ground that personal dignity, so much as the fact of being created in God's own image and likeness (cf. Genesis 1:26–27) and, even more so, being children of God...

This is not just an abstract doctrine. For Francis it is the key to a burning contemporary issue:

> We ourselves need to see, and then to enable others to see, that migrants and refugees do not only represent a problem to be solved, but are brothers and sisters to be welcomed, respected and loved. They are an occasion that Providence gives us to help build a more just society, a

more perfect democracy, a more united country, a more
fraternal world and a more open and evangelical Christian
community. Migration can offer possibilities for a new
evangelization, open vistas for the growth of a new humanity foreshadowed in the paschal mystery: a humanity
for which every foreign country is a homeland and every
homeland is a foreign country. (**MESSAGE FOR THE WORLD
DAY OF MIGRANTS AND REFUGEES, 2014. SEE PHILIPPIANS
3:20; 1 PETER 2:11; HEBREWS 13:14**)

This is the relationship we celebrate in Eucharist. Eucharist puts
us into the real world, the world where God is our Father and we
are his children—brothers and sisters to one another. All of this is
what we are saying when we pray, for ourselves and others, "Lord,
have mercy." We are saying, in part, *Lord, teach us to have mercy.*

How can we put this into practice?

The *Kyrie*—"Lord, have mercy"—reminds us to *focus on relationship* with every person we deal with, and with God. In all of
our dealings with God, we should seek conscious relationship
with one or more of the Three Persons. We may not have been
taught this. Bishop Thomas Gumbleton testifies:

> I remember back in the seminary, for twelve years, I was
> taught...that the rule expresses the will of God, so all you
> have to do is follow that and you will become holy.
>
>   What really did happen is that you learned to be a
> conformist...but in fact, that did not necessarily make you
> holy. When you conform to something without entering
> into a deeper *relationship* with the one who gives that rule
> or law—and here we're talking about the law of God—you
> simply try to follow the externals of the law and do not

understand that the law is intended to lead us to God, into a relationship with God and our brothers and sisters. ("THE PEACE PULPIT," NATIONAL CATHOLIC REPORTER, SEPTEMBER 11, 2012)

That says it all. Real holiness is *relationship*—union of heart and mind and will with God and others. We keep rules for the same reason we ask God to help us: out of an awareness of relationship. When our whole life is an awareness of interacting with other persons in loving relationship, we will know what it means to do everything "in the name of the Father, and of the Son, and of the Holy Spirit."

May "the grace of our Lord Jesus Christ, and the love of the Father, and the communion of the Holy Spirit be with you all!"

Kyrie, eleison!

For prayer and discussion

- When you say "Lord, have mercy" at Mass, are you filled with a sense of family relationship with God and others?

- When you help others who are in need, do you think, "There, but for the grace of God, go I"? Or do you think, "There, *because* of the grace of God, goes my brother or sister"?

- Does it give you confidence to pray to God as a relative?

- What would change if we all began to treat everyone else as our brothers and sisters?

CHAPTER SEVEN

"Glory to God in the highest"

The Priesthood of Praise

S uppose you had been on the street when terrorists destroyed the World Trade Center, killing thousands of office personnel, clients, firemen, policemen, and other rescue workers. Suppose someone standing in the crowd, conscious that this was an attack on the whole country, had lifted up an American flag at that moment and begun to recite the Pledge of Allegiance. Could you have joined in without tears in your eyes? Could anyone have remained silent during such a moment of intense national awareness?

The *Gloria* is like the Pledge of Allegiance. It is a moment in the Mass when we declare, not only what we believe, but what we stand for as a community of believers.

> We praise you, we bless you, we adore you, we glorify you,
> we give you thanks for your great glory...

Almost never in the "ordinary" world of social life, business, and politics do we hear any of these words. We spend our days in a world of suppressed truth and myopic understanding. Even in family life they are rarely spoken. It is shocking that in what people mistakenly call the "real" world, we almost never hear God praised. You would think that the multiplication of planets and stars, the proliferation of plants and animals, flowers and fruits of the earth all came about without any guiding intelligence, any benevolent intent on the part of any providing Person.

This is absurdity. But absurdity embraced as reality by our gullible culture of make-believe in which truth is holding its tongue.

So we sense an emphatic relief when we hear ourselves and everyone around us giving voice at Mass to what should be shouted from the housetops: *We praise you, we bless you, we adore you, we glorify you, we give you thanks for your great glory...* Finally we are taking note of the elephant in the living room. But even at Mass, we often fail to enter into the spirit of praise.

Catholics need to come alive during the *Gloria*. We need to sing. To mumble a declaration of faith is the next thing to denying it. To stand there silent while others sing the *Gloria* is to separate ourselves from the believing community. At Mass, teenagers do it all the time. In them it may be a prelude to defection.

What we praise, we will appreciate. What we do not praise, we will not appreciate. That is a law of life. If we do not listen to the words of the *Gloria*, embrace their meaning, make them our own, and praise God consciously through them, their content will depart from our minds and dissolve in our hearts. We will be "de-evangelized." We cannot "damn with faint praise" the Good News and hope to stay enthusiastic about it.

That is why we proclaim in every Mass, "It is truly right and just, *our duty and our salvation,* always and everywhere to give you thanks." Because of what we know as Christians, thanksgiving should invade our life. We know what other people do not know. We have a duty to be the voice of praise on earth. We have inherited the "priesthood of praise." Not to give God thanks and praise should be inconceivable to us.

THE PRIESTHOOD OF PRAISE

No creature on earth can praise God but humans. Psalm 148 is soaring poetically out of bounds when it says:

> Praise him, sun and moon; praise him,
>> all you shining stars!
> Praise him, you highest heavens,
>> and you waters above the heavens!...
> Wild animals and all cattle, creeping things
>> and flying birds!...
> Let them praise the name of the LORD,
>> for he commanded and they were created.
> He established them forever and ever; he fixed their
>> bounds, which cannot be passed.

None of the above can know that God "commanded and they were created," or recognize the bounds he fixed. Only humans can praise God. And therefore humans must: it is our privilege and our role in creation.

> Kings of the earth and all peoples, princes and all rulers of
>> the earth!
> Young men and women alike, old and young together!
> Let them praise the name of the LORD, for his name alone
>> is exalted; his glory is above earth and heaven.

Everything God made "goes out" from him when he speaks his creative word: "Let it be!" And everything is returned to him when humans, with wonder and praise, speak their word of recognition: "It is!"

Humans can recognize God's brilliance and admire God for it. Humans alone. That gives humans a special role. It is through humans that creation, which comes from God in the form of being, is returned to God in the form of praise and thanksgiving. These are necessary acts. Humankind is the *pontifex*, the "bridgebuilder" of praise. The greatness of a human being, Pope Francis says, "lies in being able to think of God." And in being able, because of that, to "live a conscious and responsible *relationship* with him."

This is what makes the *Gloria* so important at Mass. Conscious *relationship* with God does not exist in the world unless human beings *know* God and express what they know in praise. In singing praise and giving thanks to God, all present, as representatives of the human race, are fulfilling their duty of putting creation into recognized relationship with God. This is to accept the human responsibility—and privilege—of "bridging the gap" between unconscious, unthinking, unaware, inanimate nature and God.

This gives us a fresh look at the Mass. We now see that proclaiming the *Gloria* is an act of cosmic significance. It is to do what only humans can do. It is to be a bridge between creation and God. It is to pay creation's debt of praise. It is to recognize, accept, and embrace a fundamental duty that is a dimension of human existence. "It is...*our duty and our salvation*...to give you thanks" and praise. To join in the liturgy's hymn of praise during the *Gloria* is to become a "*pontifex* of praise."

To "single out for grateful remembrance"

We gather on Sundays to celebrate "Eucharist," which in Greek means "thanksgiving." To "celebrate" means to "single out for grateful remembrance." The *Gloria* singles out what we have to be thankful for in the Good News. We are grateful, first of all, simply for what God is: "We give you thanks for your great glory." We thank God just for being the kind of God he is.

We are grateful because we *know God*: not just in the transcendent mystery of his separateness as *"Lord God,"* but also as the God who entered history to guide and govern the Jews as his special people: *"heavenly King."* And now, because of Jesus, who became one of us to make us one with God, we know God with the closeness of sons and daughters: "almighty God and *Father*!" We praise God for the progressive intimacy of his relationship with the human race.

We give thanks because we know Jesus, who, though he was *"Lord God"* and *"Son of the Father,"*

> did not regard equality with God as something to be exploited, but emptied himself, taking the form of a slave, being born in human likeness...and became obedient to the point of death—even death on a cross.

He offered himself as *"Lamb of God"* to *"take away the sins of the world."*

> Therefore God also highly exalted him and gave him the name that is above every name, so that at the name of Jesus every knee should bend, in heaven and on earth and under the earth, and every tongue should confess that Jesus Christ is Lord, to the glory of God the Father! (**Philippians 2:6–11**)

We need to recognize the mystery here. Our sins are not just "forgiven," but "taken away." Forgiveness doesn't change the one forgiven. If God only forgives us, we are just as bad and guilty as before. But as "Lamb of God," Jesus was made to "be sin" by taking us, with all of our sins, into his body. Then he died so that we might die in him—and our sins be annihilated, "taken away" in death. Jesus "became sin" so that we might become "the very holiness of God." He "gave himself up" for us, "in order to make us holy by cleansing us…so as to present the Church to himself in splendor, without a spot or wrinkle or anything of the kind—yes, so that she may be holy and without blemish." By dying on the cross with Christ and in Christ in baptism, we rise as a "new creation." (See these key texts: Philippians 2:6; Romans 6:3; 2 Corinthians 5:21; Ephesians 5:25.)

Now Jesus is "seated at the right hand of the Father" where he can "receive our prayer" and "have mercy on us." That is something to praise and thank God for. We do it in every Mass. *"We give you thanks for your great glory."* But how enthusiastically?

Reflecting on the Second Book of Samuel, in which "David danced with all his might before the Lord," Pope Francis said this in a homily (January 28, 2014):

> David's prayer of praise led him to move beyond all reserves. His prayer became exultant…It became the prayer of praise and of joy, and he began to dance. This was a real prayer of praise.
>
> Some might think that this kind of prayer is only for those who belong to the Charismatic Renewal, not for all Christians. No. The prayer of praise is a Christian prayer for all of us. And it does not matter if we are good singers.

You are able to shout out when your team scores a goal, and you are not able to sing praises to the Lord? You can't come out of your shell ever so slightly to sing his praise?

It is easy to understand a prayer of petition—asking something of the Lord—and prayer of thanksgiving, as well. Even prayer of adoration is not so difficult to understand. Prayer of praise, however, does not come to us so easily.

Here is a good question for us to pose to ourselves today: How am I doing with the prayer of praise? Do I know how to praise the Lord? Do I praise him when I pray the *Gloria*? Is my whole heart really in it, or do I merely mouth the words?

What does David dancing here say to me? When David returned to the palace, his wife Michal, the daughter of King Saul, scolded him: "How could you have done this, you the king, dancing in front of everyone? Are you not ashamed?" Michal despised David. The Bible says that, because of this, Michal remained sterile for the rest of her life.

What does the Word of God mean here? It means that joy, that the prayer of praise, makes us fruitful! That man or woman who praises the Lord, who prays praising the Lord, and who, when praying the *Gloria* is filled with joy at doing so, is a fruitful person."

On the other hand, those who close themselves up in the formality of a prayer that is cold and restrained may end up like Michal, in the sterility of their formality.

Imagine David dancing, "with all his might before the Lord," and think how beautiful it is to make the prayer of praise.

Could it be that a parish that is "cold and restrained" in its celebration of Eucharist "may end up like Michal, in the sterility of their formality," unable to pass the life of faith on to their children?

If we take a fresh look at the *Gloria*, and bring a fresh attitude to it when we sing, we will be filled with joy and communicate that joy to others. By giving life to the liturgy, we will give life to one another.

For prayer and discussion

- On your way to Mass, are you consciously thinking of praising God?

- Do you get caught up in praising God enthusiastically during Mass?

- How enthusiastic are teenagers at Mass? Do they get this from their elders?

- Do you think you will praise God more enthusiastically at Mass after reading this?

- In Africa, people dance up to communion. Would you be willing to do that?

CHAPTER EIGHT

"You Alone are the Holy One"
We Break With Idols

> You alone are the Holy One, you alone are the Lord, you
> alone are the Most High, Jesus Christ, with the Holy Spirit,
> in the glory of God the Father...

This is our *"Shema Israel,"* our affirmation of the "greatest and first Commandment": "Hear, O Israel: The LORD is our God, the LORD alone. You shall love the Lord your God with all your heart, and with all your soul, and with all your mind."

This is the rallying call of monotheism. It recognizes the awesome mystery of an infinite God, a God without limits, unparalleled, undivided, in whom "all things in heaven and on earth were created...who is before all things, and in whom all things hold together." He is the "one God and Father of all, who is above all and through all and in all" (see Deuteronomy 6:4–5, Colossians 1:16–17; Ephesians 4:6).

The *Gloria* brings us back to the glorious height and rock-bottom foundation of our lives: God is God. God alone. And we are God's people. Our life is to be loyal. We affirm it (see Deuteronomy 4:4; Matthew 22:37).

Idolatry is commonplace in every culture. We don't burn incense to false gods; we just give them priority in our choices. Business comes before pleasure and pleasure comes before prayer. We might miss Sunday Mass, but never soccer practice. The anthropologists who dig up our ruins ten thousand years from now will probably speculate that the focus of family worship, our civilization's "household god," was the television set. In our use of time and space, we give precedence to other things over religious activities. This is idolatry.

But the *Gloria* calls us back to focus: "You alone are the Holy One, you alone are the Lord, you alone are the Most High, Jesus Christ, with the Holy Spirit, in the glory of God the Father..."

Our society is characterized by a reluctance to be absolute about anything. We hesitate to say that anything is simply wrong, period. Or that anything is absolutely true, without the shadow of a doubt. We say, "This is what I believe, but I don't say anyone else should." When the question is raised about killing a child of God who has been convicted of murder, or about the need for permanent commitment in sexual relations, or about taking the life of an unborn human being, or enlisting in the military during an unjust war, we go along— in practice, at least—with the "culture of relativism," which assumes there are no absolute moral principles and swiftly chastises even the appearance of imposing one's own opinion on anyone.

The *Gloria* does not take up particular issues or enter into the field of morality at all. Instead, it goes to the root of all morality and affirms absolutely, emphatically, and with an exclusivity that is almost embarrassing, that God is God. And God alone is

God. And nothing has the right to even lift up its voice in the same ballpark with God: "You alone are the Holy One. You alone are the Lord. You alone are the Most High!" Every human act must be measured against the transcendent standard of God's holiness, against God's right to absolute, total obedience. God's position is so high, so far above every created being, goal, value, or desire, that nothing could ever get close enough even to compete with God...not even soccer practice.

When Pope Francis was asked by journalist Eugenio Scalfari whether the church believes in "absolute truth," he answered the way Saint Ignatius told his Jesuits to answer: by "going in the other person's door and coming out your own."

> You ask me if it is an error or a sin to say that no absolute exists and therefore there is no absolute truth but only a series of relative or subjective truths.
>
> To begin with, I will not speak, not even to one who believes, of "absolute" truth, in the sense that "absolute" is what is deprived of any relationship.

Watch this Jesuit go! He just switched the focus from *relativism* to *relationship*. That brings the Trinity into the picture! God is Existence itself, the ground of all Being. But God, though One in Nature, is able to exist as Three Persons because of the different *relationships* between Father, Son, and Spirit. Therefore, since all existence is based on God's, and the very existence of God is relationship, we can't speak of anything God made as if it had no relationship with anything else! That's what you get when you think like a Jesuit!

Next, since Scalfari asked what the church believes, Francis goes to the core of all Christian belief and shows how everything else is inseparable from that:

> Now what is true, according to the Christian faith, is the
> love of God for us in Jesus Christ. Therefore, truth is a
> relationship! So true is this that when any one of us takes
> up the truth and expresses it, that expression comes from
> him or herself: from his or her history and culture, from
> the situation in which he or she lives, etc.
>
> This doesn't mean that truth is variable or subjective,
> quite the opposite. But it means that it is given to us always
> and only as a *way* and a *life*. Did not Jesus himself say:
> "I am the Way, the Truth, and the Life"? In other words,
> truth, being altogether one with love, requires humili-
> ty and openness to be sought, received and expressed.
> Therefore, it's necessary to understand one another well on
> the terms... (*LA REPUBBLICA*, SEPTEMBER 4, 2013)

Look how Francis has clarified the terms. He went in the theoret-
ical door of "absolute truth" as an abstract idea philosophers love
to play with, and came out through the practical door of truth
as "way" and "life," truth lived in action, truth as concrete perception and response—of both mind and will—to the real world
of people and things. This truth is an activity, a relationship, an
interaction with what is "out there." And if we don't perceive
what is out there according to what it really is, our relationship
will be false and destructive. It will not be love.

So yes, it is very important to see things as they really are.
Ultimately, that means to see them as God does. So if God has
told us how he sees any reality, and how we should interact with
it, that is a non-negotiable. "You alone are the Holy One. You alone
are the Lord. You alone are the Most High!" Jesus alone, God made

flesh, is the Way. Jesus alone is the Truth. Jesus alone is the Life.

When we pray the *Gloria,* we stand in the breach against the idolatry of relating to anything without seeing it in the light of its true relationship to God.

In practice, this is the way of authentic love.

For prayer and discussion

- Is there anything in your life that you do without asking how it helps you to know, love, and serve God? Would you call this an "idol"?

- All jokes aside, are you more committed to "soccer practice" (whatever form that takes for you) than you are to Sunday Mass? What are you teaching your children to put first in life?

- How many things in your life take priority over private prayer? Over family prayer? Scripture reading? Making retreats? Attending talks or devotions in your parish? Spending time discussing religion with your children? Doing volunteer work as ministry?

- Do you accompany your children in their prayer life and spiritual journey as closely as you accompany them in their athletic and artistic activities?

- What moral values do you defend as absolute? Do they include love? Prayer? Praising God? Spreading the Good News? Trying to change the world?

CHAPTER NINE

The "Presidential Prayers"
Experiencing Priesthood

Mass is a time when the church leads us to come out of ourselves and pray for each other—and to pray officially as "priests in the Priest," anointed in baptism to the ministry of prayer and sacrifice. In the three prayers that change in every Mass—the Collect (opening prayer), the Prayer over the Gifts, and the Prayer after Communion—we pray as priests for the whole church. And the liturgy guides us to pray for what really counts.

Does this give a fresh view of the Mass?

It is a principle of the spiritual life that we grow in grace (the life of God) by letting grace *express* itself in and through our human actions. We grow in faith by expressing faith in prayer and choices. We grow in hope and love the same way. When we express love for others by praying for them, we grow in love for them. Jesus taught this as a way we can even come to love those who hurt us: "Love your enemies and pray for those who persecute you"; "bless those who curse you, pray for those who abuse you" (Matthew 5:44; Luke 6:28).

Usually we pray to God for our personal desires—for our family and friends, and for particular people whose special needs have been brought to our attention. This is love—for ourselves and for others. It is also the expression, and therefore the experience, of faith and trust in God.

At Mass we broaden our perspective and pray for the whole church. This makes us grow in a special love for the whole community of faith by praying in an all-inclusive way for everyone who believes. We do this by joining in the "presidential prayers." These prayers do three things:

- they express the special love for one another that bonds us to each other as a community of faith;

- they teach us what to pray for, and in this way teach us what to live for;

- they remind us of our identity as *priests* anointed in baptism to pray for others and to offer the sacrifice of Christ.

Why are they called "presidential prayers"?

The *General Instruction of the Roman Missal*, 30, explains:

> Among those things assigned to the [presiding] Priest...
> are the orations: that is to say, the Collect [Opening
> Prayer], the Prayer over the Offerings, and the Prayer after
> Communion. These prayers are addressed to God by the
> priest who presides over the assembly...in the name of the
> entire holy people and of all present. Hence, they are right-

ly called the "presidential prayers."

The truth is, these are not really prayers the priest says "in the name" of the community. They are the prayers of the assembly itself that the ordained priest "presides" over as "president of the assembly," hence "presidential." They are the assembly's prayers that everyone present is praying. That is why they are always in the plural: "God our Father, *we* ask...grant to *us*..." The presiding priest is just the one who says the words out loud.

If we are not precise in our terminology, we get misled. The official liturgical instructions strive for precision, but not consistently enough to erase from the Catholic mind the misconceptions that centuries of inaccurate terminology have implanted in us. We need to correct one of those before we go on. In our restricted and unorthodox understanding, the word "priest" has come to mean for us someone who has received the sacrament of holy orders, someone who has been officially ordained as priest. This is a distortion of Catholic doctrine.

As Bishop Patrick Dunn, bishop of Auckland, has noted, Vatican II tried to clarify things by "avoiding terms such as 'clergy' and 'priest,' and by returning to the New Testament expression 'presbyter' with its collegial and fraternal associations. As a general rule, the conciliar texts try to follow the Scriptures and to restrict the word 'priest' (*sacerdos*) to Jesus himself and to the 'common priesthood' of the baptized; and when talking about the ordained they use the word '*presbyteros*.' But the English translation uncritically translates both '*sacerdos*' and '*presbyteros*' as 'priest.'" Thus, the effort to correct the terminology failed. (See Patrick Dunn, *Priesthood: A Re-Examination of the Roman Catholic Theology of the Presbyterate* [Alba House, 1990], pp. 77 ff.)

Catholics affirm, in agreement with the Letter to the Hebrews (chapters 5-10), that ever since Jesus offered himself as priest and victim on Calvary, there is only one Priest: Jesus himself. All other priesthood is abolished.

For Christians, the only way to be a "priest" is to be a "priest in the Priest" by incorporation into Christ, becoming a member of Christ's own body through baptism. When we "become Christ" by baptism, we become what he is—including what he is uniquely. For example, Jesus is the *"only* Son" of the Father. However, we are true "sons and daughters *in the Son."* Likewise, Jesus is the *only* priest. But we are "priests *in the Priest."* This is through baptism, not by holy orders, and it is the fundamental Christian priesthood: the priesthood of all those who are baptized "into Christ" and therefore into his priesthood. That is why the bishops at Vatican II tried to reserve the word "priest" for those who are priests by baptism, and use "presbyter" for one with holy orders.

Holy orders does add something. It adds empowerment to particular *functions* of Christ's priesthood that are not common to all the baptized. When the official documents say that the priesthood of the ordained is "essentially different" from that given by baptism, they are not denying that there is only one unique priesthood of Jesus that has replaced all others. There is only one priesthood, in which the baptized and the ordained all share alike. But within that priesthood there are functions that only holy orders empowers one to perform. That is the difference between them.

We might compare this difference to the distinction between the Three Persons of the Trinity, who have one and the same nature as God, but differ as Persons by their relationships—which are determined by their different ways of *interacting* with each other. Saint Paul says that in the church, the one body of Christ, "there are varieties of gifts, but the same Spirit; and there are varieties of services, but the same Lord; and there are varieties of activities, but it is the same God who activates all of them in everyone" (1 Corinthians 12:4-6). None of these gifts or functions makes anyone "higher" or "lower," or in any way "more" or "less" than anyone else. In this, all Christians are like the Three Persons of the Trinity: "equal in majesty, undivided in splendor." We all have equal dignity and prestige, but we differ in the kinds of service we render to one another. We are all equal as one body of Christ, and the same Spirit acts in and through us all, but we differ in the ways we interact with each other according to each one's role.

The point is that the priesthood of holy orders, although from a particular point of view it is sometimes called "higher," is nevertheless secondary to that of baptism. One has to be baptized before one can be ordained. And holy orders simply adds a function to the priesthood one already has. The basic, fundamental Christian priesthood is the priesthood in which all participate who have become "priests in the Priest" by being baptized "into Christ." *

[* *Since the power to perform the functions of holy orders is given permanently, we can say it becomes part of the ordained priest's "being," in the same way that a kidney transplant becomes part of the receiver's body and being. This allows us to say that ordination to the priesthood of holy orders brings about an "ontological change" (a change of being) in the one ordained. It does, because he now has the permanent power to exercise certain functions. But it does not make the priest some kind of "super Christian," higher and better than others. To think like that is clericalism.*]

Pope Francis spoke to this in *The Joy of the Gospel*, 104:

> It must be remembered that [in the words of John Paul II,
> *Christifideles Laici* (30 December 1988), no. 51] when we
> speak of sacramental power "we are in the realm of func-
> tion, not that of dignity or holiness." The ministerial priest-
> hood is one means employed by Jesus for the service of his
> people, yet our great dignity derives from baptism, which
> is accessible to all. The configuration of the priest to Christ
> the head—namely, as the principal source of grace—does
> not imply an exaltation which would set him above others.
> In the Church, functions "do not favor the superiority of
> some vis-à-vis the others."

That is why it is misleading to say that the ordained priest "says"
Mass, "offers" Mass, "celebrates" Mass, or (in Spanish) "gives" the
Mass. Those terms implicitly reduce the assembly to "hearing" or
"receiving" the Mass as something the ordained priest offers and
celebrates while they watch him do it. The *General Instruction
of the Roman Missal* is explicit about this: "The meaning of this
[Eucharistic] Prayer is that the *whole congregation* of the faithful
joins with Christ in confessing the great deeds of God and in the
offering of Sacrifice" (no. 78). In the eucharistic celebration, the
correct word for the ordained priest is the "presider" or "president of the assembly." That tells us that what is taking place
is the work of the whole assembly. You cannot "preside" over
something you are doing all by yourself!

So after the *Gloria*, when the presider reads out loud the
Collect (opening prayer), everyone in the assembly is fulfilling
the special duty and desire each member of the body of Christ has
to pray for the whole body. In the three "presidential prayers"—

Collect, Prayer over the Gifts, and Prayer after Communion—we never ask anything for individuals as such, only for the church and all believers. This duty and dedication to praying for all of our brothers and sisters in Christ is an element of our identity that is mostly overlooked in the unreal world of daily life. We become conscious of it in the eucharistic celebration—if we pay attention to the words.

If we pay attention to the words, they will teach us something else. Except for special "Masses for various needs and occasions," the presidential prayers seldom if ever ask for the things we ordinarily ask God for: health, protection, success in what we are doing, and other things that enhance our human life in this world. A sample of the Collect prayers for the first Sundays of Advent, Lent, Easter, and Pentecost shows the Mass focusing us on more important priorities (these prayers are taken from the pastoral translation of the 1985 Sacramentary in preference to the Roman-English Missal of 2011):

> All-powerful God, increase our strength of will for doing good, that Christ may find an eager welcome at his coming....
>
> Father, through our observance of Lent, help us to understand the meaning of your Son's death and resurrection, and teach us to reflect it in our lives....
>
> God our Father, by raising Christ your Son, you conquered the power of death and opened for us the way to eternal life. Let our celebration today raise us up and renew our lives by the Spirit that is within us....
>
> God our Father, let the Spirit you sent on your Church to begin the teaching of the Gospel continue to work in the world through the hearts of all who believe....

These are not things it ordinarily occurs to us to pray for. The presidential prayers, in teaching us what we should pray for, remind us of what we should live for.

For prayer and discussion

- Do you listen closely at Mass when the presider reads the presidential prayers (Opening Prayer, Prayer over the Gifts, Prayer after Communion)? Do you sometimes need to read them ahead of time and translate them into your own words?

- Do you put your heart into asking God for what the prayers are asking? Do the prayers give you more insight into what you should desire and live for? How does this carry over after Mass?

- When you join in the presidential prayers, does it make you aware of yourself as participating officially as a priest in the eucharistic celebration? Will you be more aware of it now that you have read this?

- If so, what will that change in the way you participate in the rest of the Mass? In your daily life?

CHAPTER TEN

The Liturgy of the Word
The Living Voice of God

The Liturgy of the Word opens up an encounter with the living voice of God. During the Scripture readings at Mass we are not just listening to another human being reading to us out of a book. The Vatican II bishops were explicit about this. In the Council document *On Divine Revelation* (no. 21), they speak of a "real presence" of God in the Scriptures that they compare to the real presence of Jesus in the Eucharist:

> The Church has always venerated the divine Scriptures just as she venerates the body of the Lord, since, especially in the sacred liturgy, she unceasingly receives and offers to the faithful the bread of life from the table both of God's word and of Christ's body...They make the voice of the Holy Spirit resound in the words of the prophets and Apostles...For

in the sacred books, the Father who is in heaven *meets His children* with great love and *speaks with them.*

The *General Instruction of the Roman Missal* (29) says:

> When the Sacred Scriptures are read in the Church, *God himself speaks* to his people, and *Christ*, present in his word, *proclaims the Gospel.*

It would not be inappropriate if we listened to the Scripture readings on our knees!

We come into church out of a world where we are constantly bombarded with lies, "spin," false assumptions, and philosophies. We live in a "secular" culture where, sometimes by law and more commonly by mutual consent, religious truths are denied public expression. We absorb distorted values and false attitudes so unconsciously that for the most part we do not even call them into question.

Then we enter into the real world of the eucharistic celebration and hear the word of God. It is the word of all Three Persons. The words of the Father, Son, and Spirit are reality.

God's word is the truth that makes us free (John 8:32). But we have to *respond* to it. The Scripture readings at Mass are meant to be an interaction between living persons. Our listening is more than just paying attention. It is a two-way act of communication between ourselves and God, a conversation that is not authentic unless we are actively engaged in it.

We listen, not as an audience but as an assembly. We are gathered together to make ourselves heard in dialogue with God. We are *disciples*—which means "students," not "followers"—who are seriously trying to understand the mind and heart of God in order to know him ourselves and make him known to the world. The words Jesus told us to make our first petition in prayer and our first priority in life—"*Hallowed be thy Name*"—echo in our hearts as "background music." We listen to be able to make our Father known and loved.

We listen to *learn* as *disciples*. We learn to *proclaim* as *prophets*. We proclaim to *give life* to the world as "*priests in the Priest*," offering our bodies as a "living sacrifice" of self-expression to communicate faith, hope, and love to all whom we encounter: our "flesh for the life of the world."

Finally, we listen as "*kings*" or "stewards of the kingship of Christ," who have taken *responsibility* for establishing his reign over every area and activity of human life on earth. We listen to learn more clearly what we are doing, why we are doing it, and how it needs to be done. This is not the listening of an "audience" sitting back and hoping something will sink in. This is the listening of avid learners committed to "seek peace" through the pursuit of truth (Psalm 34:14; 1 Peter 3:11). It is intense. (If we want to change the world we actually love in (that was a typo: I meant to write "live in," but the mistake is better than the original), we will find an inspired set of guidelines in *The Joy of the Gospel* by Pope Francis, chapter four, "The Social Dimension of Evangelization." He covers all the dimensions.

A MATTER OF PERSPECTIVE

To absorb the truth of the mind and heart of God revealed in Scripture, we have to understand how God speaks. Then we have to reflect on God's words.

Many "pre-Vatican II Catholics" grew up assuming that God wrote the Scriptures like the daily news. God's words meant whatever they would mean if we read them in an American newspaper. If God said Jonah was swallowed by a whale, that was gospel truth, not a fish story. God can't lie, so whatever he says must be true.

From this overly simplistic perspective, we assume that the images of God we find in Scripture are like photographs—"what you see is what you get." If God speaks angry words, he is an angry God. Threatening words, he is a vengeful God. Comforting words, he is a merciful God. If he says he is going to punish, he is going to punish, and he'll do it just the way he says he will.

But the images are inconsistent. It is no wonder that people sometimes saw God as schizophrenic: on good days, no one could be nicer; on bad days, no one could be more cruel. It was confusing. And it produced schizophrenic Christians who sought out "sweet Jesus" in times of trouble, but dreaded to meet him at death.

So let's get this straight. The truth God reveals is divine; but his way of revealing it is human. In the Bible, God talks to people the way people talk to each other: sometimes in factual reporting (John 19:16), sometimes in wild exaggerations (1 Kings 4:20–34), sometimes in images straight out of science fiction (Revelation 12:3), sometimes like a parent threatening a child with the "bogey man" (Mark 9:43). These are all *literary forms*, and, depending on the form the writer is using, we interpret God's words literally or figuratively.

Scripture paints many images of God, and they are interpretative portraits, not photographs. They are more like a series of vignettes, showing different aspects of God from different angles. To interpret what the inspired writer is showing us, we have to know the particular point of view he is taking, what characteristics of God he wants to highlight, and what he is leaving out of the picture.

In the Bible, God comes across sometimes like a loving Father (Luke 15:22), sometimes as a ruthless judge (Matthew 25:41), sometimes as an erotic lover (Song of Songs 4:1), sometimes like a vengeful tyrant (Luke 19:27), a greedy capitalist (Luke 19:22), a marketplace negotiator (Genesis 18:24), or a racist (Matthew 15:26). With Peter, Jesus was fierce (Matthew 16:23). With John, he was gentle (John 13:23). With a woman caught in adultery, he was all compassion (John 8:11). With the Pharisees, his rage could be vicious (Matthew, chapter 23).

How we interpret the Bible depends a lot on how comfortable we are with God, and on how aware we are that you have to take God's words the way God means them, not always at face value. We have to imagine the expression on his face when he said them (picture Jesus looking up at Zacchaeus in Luke 19:5). The more we know God, the better we will understand the Bible. And the better we understand the Bible, the more we will know God.

The Liturgy of the Word reminds us of this. If we listen to the readings, it gets us started. It encourages us to extend our Scripture reading at home, where we can take time to reflect, to meditate on what we have read, and to decide what we will do about it. In fact, the *General Instruction of the Roman Missal* (nos. 29, 56) specifies that "the Liturgy of the Word is to be celebrated in such a way as to *favor meditation...*" by means of which, "under the action of the Holy Spirit, the Word of God may be grasped by the heart and a response through prayer may be prepared."

These are the "three Rs" of Scriptural prayer: *reading, reflection,* and *response.* Together they form a three-legged stool: leave any leg off, and the other two fall with it. Then our claim to be "disciples" doesn't have a leg to stand on.

If we decide to do so, we can read Scripture. We can meditate on God's words. And if we respond in choices, we will be changed by them. Jesus said "to the Jews who had believed in him: 'If you continue in my word, you are truly my disciples; and you will *know the truth,* and the truth will *make you free'*" (John 8:31–32).

On the other hand, if we choose not to look for light in the real world, we will be slaves to the phony one. That is the decision that faces us: to give up looking for understanding of the world, of ourselves, and of God by turning our minds over to the culture or to accept enlightenment from God. You would think the choice is obvious.

Once we start reading Scripture, we find that the Truth of God is too vast to compress into doctrines, no matter how perfectly worded they are. And the goodness of God cannot be codified in rules, no matter how good and necessary they are. We become *disciples*; we become *students*. We are launched into a life of constant change.

So make yourself a rule. But don't call it a rule; call it a "personal commitment," a "covenant" between yourself and Jesus. Enter into a new relationship with him. Promise to be his student if he will be your teacher.

Then you will find the Liturgy of the Word a fresh experience every time you use it to encounter the living God.

For prayer and discussion

- What was last week's gospel about? Did you make any changes in your life after hearing it?

- Do you listen to the readings at Mass with a sense of awe that God is speaking to you right now?

- Are you committed to reading Scripture regularly? Can you make that commitment now?

- How hard would it be to discuss with one or two others what you have read, felt, and responded to in Scripture? Are you willing to take the initiative in starting such a relationship?

CHAPTER ELEVEN

The Homily
An Interactive Conversation

e should be grateful for homilies. How many times in an ordinary week does someone talk to us about the most important things in life, using the words of God as a guide?

The fact that there are homilies on Sunday is a triumph of church leadership. Before the Protestant Reformation many priests were either too ignorant to preach (there were no seminaries) or didn't bother. The Council of Trent (1545-1563) reacted to this by making it a rule: "There is to be a homily on Sundays and holy days of obligation at all Masses."

But a homily does us very little good if we just sit back to enjoy it! What we get out of a homily depends more on us than it does on the homilist.

Remember that whoever is preaching is just a fellow student like ourselves. Jesus said to his disciples, "Do not let yourselves be called teachers; for one is your teacher, the Christ" (Matthew

23:10). All those who stand up to teach or preach are just fellow classmates giving back what they have heard Christ the teacher say. We need to see if what they say matches what we have heard, sitting at the feet of the same teacher and listening likewise to his words.

Homilies are not sermons or lectures; they are *sharing*. The word "homily" comes from the Greek verb *homilein*, which means to "interact verbally" with a person. If we don't interact, it is not a homily. Then, whether we are bored or entertained, our participation in that moment of the Mass has not been authentic.

Verbal interaction about the homily doesn't usually take place at Mass. But there should be verbal interaction after Mass. We should discuss with each other what we hear—and give feedback to the homilist if possible. Without feedback, the preacher doesn't know if he is feeding the flock or not. He might be preaching in a vacuum. Or preaching error! If he does that once, it is his fault. If he does it twice because no one has informed him, it is the congregation's fault. If the congregation interacts with him and he still keeps doing it, it is everybody's fault. The congregation should insist that he get help or let someone else preach. Pope Francis wrote: "The homily is the touchstone for judging a pastor's closeness and ability to communicate to his people." But communication is a two-way street.

It takes two to tango. If the congregation doesn't do its part, the quality of the homilies will decline until, in the words of Francis, "the laity will suffer from having to listen to them and the clergy from having to preach them!" But if preacher and people both do their part, "the homily can actually be an intense and happy experience of the Spirit, a consoling encounter with God's word, a constant source of renewal and growth" (*The Joy of the Gospel*, no. 135).

At Mass, we are not an audience just sitting back hoping for something to happen. We are *disciples*—students, active learners, intent on "getting something" out of the readings and homily. We can always do this by interacting with what is said on a personal and private level. And everyone should. But how? The best way is to read the readings ourselves before we come to Mass. Perhaps read them with our family a little at a time during supper. Or over the phone with a friend. Think about them. Talk about them. Then see if at Mass the homilist matches or improves on what we saw in the readings. (For the daily readings, go to *www.usccb.org /bible/readings.*)

The most certain way to "get something" out of the readings and the homily is to listen for something we believe God is saying to us that we can *respond* to—in decisions, in *action*. Just the choice to believe what we hear is an action—if we make it consciously, explicitly, and deliberately. But we should always try to find some physical action, something we can do that *expresses* our belief. If we do this at every Mass, we are making the homily happen. We are interacting. Why not decide you will never leave church after Mass until you have come to some decision, no matter how small, in response to what you have heard?

We need to take a fresh look at the homily. If we do, we may find ourselves hearing things at Mass we have never heard or noticed before. Then we will have something to carry out to others. If we "interact verbally" with friends and family about what we have heard, we will be extending the homily to the world outside.

That is evangelization.

For prayer and discussion

- What do you remember from last week's homily?

- Did you listen for what Jesus himself was saying to you in it?

- Did you interact with it? Did you summarize it in your own mind afterwards? Did you ask if anything in it challenged you or inspired you?

- Did you come to any *decision* as a result of what you heard in the readings and homily?

- What decision will you make in response to what you have just read?

CHAPTER TWELVE

The Profession of Faith

The Point Is, We Profess

I t is a glorious thing to stand up after the reading of God's word and profess our faith. We experience our being. We have minds: we understand. We have wills: we choose to accept. We are self-determining persons. God speaks, and we answer. We declare ourselves in response to what we have heard: "*We believe.*"

The emphasis is not on *what* we believe, but on the fact that we believe it.

The Profession of Faith can be a mystical experience, that is, a moment in which we become aware of the mystery in what we are professing and of the mystery involved in the fact that we can profess it. No one can believe the truths we profess in the Creed except by the divine gift of faith, the gift of sharing in God's own knowing act. "Faith" is the divine gift of knowing what only God can know as only God can know it. To recite the Profession of Faith with *awareness* of this is to experience *enlightenment* by

72

the Holy Spirit.

It is also to experience Christian solidarity in the "communion of the Holy Spirit." We are united. We stand together. We support each other in professing truths that we know by divine enlightenment. We are Christians because we have received the word of God from the Father through Jesus, and we understand it by the gift of the Spirit.

Sometimes we feel alone in our faith. To profess it aloud with others supports us.

It would be false to assume that no one else in our culture takes God seriously. Most human beings throughout the world believe in God. And they always have, since the beginning of time. Depending on the statistics you read, eighty-four percent of the world's population believes in God (under some form). About a third of those (over two billion) are Christians, and about half the Christians are Catholic. The Nicene Creed that we profess at Mass forms the mainstream definition of Christianity for Catholics, Eastern Orthodox, Episcopalians, Lutherans, Methodists, Presbyterians, and the great majority of Protestant denominations.

But you would not know this from just living and working in our society. Nonbelievers have largely succeeded in giving their "tone" to our society. Why? Because many of them act and speak in public and in private as if the absence of faith and faith-inspired values is taken for granted, while believers remain silent.

It is the norm on TV that the "good guys" never pray, never set foot in a church, use God's name as a cuss word, engage in uncommitted sex, rejoice in taking revenge, and without hesitation kill the "bad guys." Religion, if not caricatured, is ignored. It just isn't "out there." Jesus Christ is never mentioned except as a swear word. (We should insist that the civil right of free speech does not include a moral right to blaspheme anybody's God in public!) Judging from the culture, Jesus isn't a player.

But the truth is, he is "in there" in the hearts of almost 250 million persons just in the U.S. alone, and just counting Christians. That is 79.5% of the population. However, they are the "silent majority." Christians just don't *profess* their faith unless they are in church, and then they do it in a low voice, without much sign of conviction. A fresh look at the Profession of Faith should motivate us to change this.

Instead of focusing on what we are professing—which we have heard a thousand times before and assume, perhaps rashly, that we understand—we should put our hearts into the fact we are professing it. We need to get in touch with our faith, not with *what* we believe, but with the fact that we believe it. During the Profession of Faith we should experience intensely our identity as believers by expressing intensely the truths that together we accept and affirm. Experience reaches awareness in expression.

If we experience ourselves intensely as believers during the eucharistic liturgy, it should become easier for us to express ourselves as believers outside of it. If we choose to do this, we can have a transforming effect on our culture—at least on that part of it we are involved in.

For prayer and discussion

- Do you listen to what you are saying during the Profession of Faith? Do you ask about anything you don't understand?

- Do you feel you are taking a personal stand when you recite the words? Do you feel good about that?

- Does expressing your faith in unity with the whole community strengthen you to express and live what you believe outside of church?

- Can you think of some concrete ways you might do that?

CHAPTER THIRTEEN

The Prayer of the Faithful

We Bring the Whole World to the Table

I t is a human function, a role implicit in being human, not only to praise God but to pray to God for ourselves and others. We do this—and accept it as an element of our human and Christian identity—when we join in the Universal Prayer or Prayer of the Faithful. The words to notice are "universal" and "of the faithful."

By the word "universal," the church is trying to get us beyond shortsighted concern for our own well-being and that of our limited circle of family and friends. The point of the Universal Prayer is to express and experience our solidarity with the suffering of the whole human race.

This is called the *Prayer of [all] the Faithful,* because it is a prayer in which the laity consciously exercise their baptismal priesthood by praying for the needs of the human race. It is important to note first that the hierarchy, as official spokesmen for the church, do not determine what we pray for here. The people in the assembly do. Second, we are not just praying for fellow believers, but for everyone and everything the people present are encountering in their daily lives. Vatican II's *Dogmatic Constitution on the Church* (31) explains that "the laity, by their very vocation...live in the 'world,' that is, in each and in all of the secular professions and occupations. They live in the ordinary circumstances of family and social life, from which the very web of their existence is woven." So the laity are the ones most in touch with what is "out there" that we need to pray for. This means the intentions should come out of the congregation—whether collected beforehand and read out, or voiced spontaneously from the pews. The intentions are the prayer of the *faithful*.

Catholic tradition recognized participation in this prayer during Mass as the special privilege of those anointed as priests by baptism. For this reason, catechumens did not join in until they were baptized and shared in Eucharist for the first time. Then they were able to stand before God as priests divinely consecrated to plead on behalf of the whole human race, fulfilling, as part of their liturgical role, a duty that, like praise, is not only Christian but cosmic.

When we hear the members of the assembly bringing to God all the needs, sufferings, and problems they are encountering in the "outside" world, we know we are adding a needed ingredient to human life. We are not just standing by as silent and helpless spectators. We are responding. There is an old country western song that begins, "I saw the wreck on the highway, but I didn't hear nobody pray." At Mass we hear it.

For prayer and discussion

- What do you bring to the Prayer of the Faithful? Do you present for prayer the needs and suffering you have seen during the week?

- Does it impress you to see during the Prayer of the Faithful how much love and concern others are showing?

- Does the Prayer of the Faithful expand your horizons by inviting you to pray for people or problems you may not have thought of?

CHAPTER FOURTEEN

The Presentation of the Gifts
We Pledge Ourselves

T he Presentation of the Gifts makes us aware that humans can, and are called to, do what is divine. We have a mission to transform the world. We ourselves have been transformed so that we might do it. To express this, we bring up bread and wine as "gifts" to be transformed into the Body and Blood of Christ. They are symbols of the gift we made of ourselves at baptism, when we were transformed by being identified with Jesus Christ. We "present" them, and present ourselves, as a renewal of our pledge to live and work as Christ's body on earth.

This lifts up to a higher plane our cultural view of work and life. People think that by working for a living and putting food on the table they are keeping themselves alive. And they are, in a very tenuous and temporary way that is totally provisional. But at the Presentation of Gifts, people bring up bread and wine and place them on the altar to be transformed into the true Bread of Life and into the Blood of the "new and everlasting covenant." This brings us into reality—the reality of the "true bread" that

79

"comes down from heaven and gives life to the world." To work for this bread is to gain the eternal life promised by the unbreakable word of God (John 6:31–33). This is the real world. It is greater than anything the world outside of church—the world that seems so normal to us—even hints of.

There is more. In the "outside" world, we think we understand the limitations of cause and effect. Human efforts produce human results. You can't make a silk purse out of a sow's ear. But in the real world of Eucharist, we are made conscious that God uses created things to produce divine effects. The "fruit of the earth and work of human hands" becomes the "Bread of Life." The "fruit of the vine" becomes our "spiritual drink." And when the "water" of our humanity is mixed with the "wine" of Christ's divinity, Jesus works *with us, in us,* and *through us,* his human creatures, to produce divine fruit, to give divine life, through all of our human words and actions. To celebrate this mystery is to become conscious of the real world, the world we actually live in.

The bread and wine we present are symbols of ourselves. To show this, they are brought up through the whole congregation, and there should be a host on the plate for each person present. This invites us to present our bodies "as a living sacrifice...to God" (Romans 12:1) as we were presented on the day of our baptism. If we were infants at the time—or even if we weren't—the Presentation of Gifts invites us to "re-up," to reaffirm our baptism by putting ourselves symbolically on the altar with the bread and wine to be transformed. We declare our free and conscious participation in the sacrifice that Jesus offered on the cross. Our baptism made us co-priests and co-victims with Jesus in that sacrifice; and during the liturgy it is made present here and now on the altar. At every Mass we "present our bodies" again, to be offered with Jesus and in Jesus for the life of the world.

To make this offering as adults is to accept the *mission* of Jesus, the mission of the church. In baptism we gave our bodies to Jesus so that he might rise from the dead in us and continue his presence and work in the world in and through our physical bodies. To do this we received the triple anointing with chrism that consecrated, committed, and empowered us to continue the messianic mission of "the Christ" ("Anointed one," "Messiah") as priest, prophet, and king.

To fulfill our mission as "prophets in the Prophet," we need to profess our faith, not just in words but in a lifestyle that cannot be explained without the presence of the risen Jesus living within us. If we visibly live by the truth and values Jesus taught in his new law (see the Sermon on the Mount, Matthew, chapters 5–7), this bears witness to the invisible life of God within us, because nothing else could make possible this divine level of behavior. It is to bear this witness that God gives us the "gift of the Holy Spirit."

Does that sound shocking? Jesus says in the Gospel of Matthew that unless our behavior is on a higher level than that of the scribes and Pharisees, we will "never enter the kingdom of heaven" (Matthew 5:20). And the Pharisees were about as moral as you can get. They kept all the rules. They didn't commit any of the sins we were taught as little children to "examine our conscience" for in preparation for confession. Oh, they might have slipped some, like all of us do, but basically the Pharisees were all "straight arrows"—the kind of people we would recognize as "observant Catholics" today. They behaved. But they rejected Jesus. Jesus calls us to live on the level of God. And he was killed for it.

Maybe we would kill him too, if we understood as well as his enemies did what he was calling for. But nobody preaches that to us. Ponder these examples for a moment. When is the last time somebody told you that you have to lend to everyone who wants to borrow something from you? That would put the bankers out of business. Or that if someone wants to sue you for anything, you should just turn over what you are being sued for and add a little more to show you have no hard feelings? That would leave half the lawyers out of work. When were you last told it is the command of Jesus that you should not resist anyone who wants to harm you? That if you try to save your earthly life by self-defense, you will lose eternal life? That would be the end of the military. But Jesus said *all* that. Read Matthew 5:38–42; 16:25.

Okay, okay, the church doesn't teach with all her authority that we are obliged to do any of those things literally. But tell me, in "ordinary life," what does the church teach as the *right* understanding of what Jesus said in those passages? Isn't it true that we just say, "Well, he didn't mean us to take those examples literally," and leave it at that? We agree on what Jesus did not mean, but we don't ask what he did mean. That leaves us with nothing more than the "righteousness of the Pharisees," which is good, normal, acceptable human behavior—the morality that Jesus rejected as not enough. For which they killed him. Jesus was put to death precisely for giving us the New Law. And the irony is that most Christians today neither reject his New Law nor accept it. We just ignore it.

CHRISTIAN WITNESS: LIVING THE NEW LAW
We can't afford to ignore the New Law. To be recognizable as the risen body of Jesus, Christians need to live visibly in a way that cannot be explained unless Jesus is living and acting in them. Christian witness begins where the Ten Commandments leave off. It begins when our behavior is so new and different—and

so good—that it raises eyebrows. This means that, if we want to embrace Christ's mission by living out our baptismal consecration as prophets, we will have to study Christ's New Law until it radically transforms our lifestyle.

Jesus' New Law calls into question not just the Law God gave to Israel, but the moral conscience of humanity itself. The Ten Commandments of the Jewish covenant are basically recognized by every rational human being as the fundamental rules for living a decent human life. What makes Christians different is that we believe they are not enough. This makes us threatening. For example, the New Law of Jesus says, "Do not resist an evildoer." That is a threat to personal, corporate, and state security. And Jesus goes into specifics: If anyone strikes you on the right cheek, turn the other also; or wants to sue you and take your coat, give your cloak as well; or forces you to go one mile, go a second mile (see Matthew 5:39–42).

The examples may sound farfetched. But the principle behind them is clear. Maintaining good relationships with other persons must be so important to Christians that it takes precedence over everything else except God. We value people, and friendship with people, more than our hurt feelings, our possessions, and our time.

Jesus goes further. He commands us: "Love your enemies and pray for those who persecute you." And his reason is "so that you may be children of your Father in heaven." With that last line, Jesus finally tells us where he is coming from. The old law gave us guidelines for living in peace with other people on earth—like good human beings. The New Law gives us guidelines for living a life that is divine—like children of God. By baptism we became children of the Father. So now we have to live by "family standards" that are divine, not just human. Jesus sums up the New

Law in one line: "Be perfect, therefore, as your heavenly Father is perfect" (Matthew 5:48).

Jesus also changed the "second greatest commandment." It is no longer "Love your neighbor as yourself." That is still based on a human standard. Jesus says, "I give you a new commandment, that you love one another just as I have loved you" (John 13:34). This calls us to be perfect as God the Son is perfect. We are to love as Jesus loves, because by baptism we "became Christ."

Paul will later bring the Third Person of the Trinity into the picture by insisting that the only way for a Christian to live a graced life is to "live by the Spirit" and "be guided by the Spirit" (Galatians 5:25). The bottom line is that for Christians the only way to live by Christ's New Law is to act divinely, "in the name of"—that is, in union with—the Trinity: Father, Son and Spirit, in everything we do.

When this level of life is visible in our physical words and actions, we are the sign and proof that Jesus has risen from the dead and is living now in us. That is Christian witness.

ACCEPTING THE MISSION

Bearing witness is what we recommit to at the Presentation of Gifts when we consciously, in symbol, place our created reality on the altar with the bread and wine to be transformed and used to do divine work on earth. Now we enter into the real world, into the truth of what we are really on earth to do, and into the mystery of our divine empowerment to do it. The "outside" world of "ordinary" life that aims only at good, human behavior is a world blind to the mystery of Christian life, a world that ignores it, a world that lives on ground level.

The Presentation of Gifts climaxes for us when we come to our feet in answer to the presider's invitation and proclaim our conscious, personal participation in what is going on at Mass. We say the words:

> May the Lord accept the sacrifice [our sacrifice]
> at your hands,
> for the praise and glory of his name,
> for our good,
> and the good of all his holy Church.

By presenting our bodies as a living sacrifice to God (see Romans 12:1), incorporated by baptism into the sacrifice of Jesus on the cross, we are committing ourselves:

> to *praise* God at Mass and live for *the praise and glory of his name* in a way that makes others praise him;

> to *try* to "get something" out of Mass by putting something into it through "full, conscious, active" participation: *"for our good"*;

> to *work* for *"the good of all his holy Church"* and of the human race that the church "exists to evangelize."

We do this by living a life of *witness*, through a lifestyle that "raises irresistible questions" in the minds of all who know us—questions that cannot be answered except through acknowledgment of the risen Jesus living within us. Now we are in touch with our real mission and the real meaning of our lives on earth. Now we are in the real world.

At every Mass, the Presentation of Gifts invites us to see ourselves as represented by the bread and wine, and in our hearts to place ourselves on the altar with them to be transformed—not on the level of *being*, since we have already "become Christ," his real body and blood, by baptism, but on the level of *action*. We place ourselves on the altar as a "living sacrifice," pledging that wherever our live body is, we will be "sacrificed" to bearing witness to the real presence of the living Jesus within us by speaking and acting always on the level of the divine life of God.

To recall this in every liturgy, making every Presentation of Gifts a moment of repeated rededication, will give us a fresh look at the Mass that, over time, will lift up the whole level of our behavior from human to divine.

For prayer and discussion

- Do you think bearing witness to Christ as described here is unrealistic?

- Could you accept to just *ask the question* about all of your choices, "How does this bear witness to the values of Christ?"

- What do you see in the words and actions of the Presentation of Gifts that you didn't see before?

CHAPTER 15

The Preface

An Interplanetary Chorus

The Preface is designed to make sure, before we move into the Eucharistic Prayer, that we are ready to enter into the heart and height of the eucharistic mystery. It begins like a mini pep rally, with the presider calling for a cheer and the congregation responding:

"The Lord be with you!"

"And with your spirit!" (We should be roaring this.)

"Lift up your hearts!"

"We lift them up to the Lord!"

"Let us give thanks to the Lord our God!"

"It is right and just!"

The presider then echoes our last words. Every preface begins
with the presider declaring, "It is truly right and just, our duty
and our salvation, always and everywhere to give you thanks,"
because...

Then each different preface describes something great—fan-
tastic, even—that God has done for us that we should thank him
for. There are eighty-four prefaces, some fitted to the seasons of
the liturgical year, some focused on particular events or truths
about God, some celebrating special moments in Christian life,
like holidays, marriage, and death. Every one of them holds up to
us something wonderful God has done and is doing, something
that might be overlooked in the distracted focus of daily life.
They all serve as a transition from ground-level consciousness
to soaring awareness of the "breadth and length and height and
depth" of God's goodness and love. They "lift up our hearts" to
prepare us for the transcendent height of the Eucharistic Prayer.

Once our minds are "lifted up" to contemplate the wonders of
God, we are ready to sing with the angels. And that is what we
do, joining our voices to the chorus of "all the heavenly hosts" to
"sing the hymn of [God's] glory":

> Holy, Holy, Holy Lord God of hosts.
> Heaven and earth are full of your glory.
> Hosanna in the highest.
> Blessed is he who comes in the name of the Lord.
> Hosanna in the highest.

The Preface takes us out of the world of ordinary life and "lifts
us up" to join the interplanetary chorus of the angels and saints

who are exulting in glory. We are ready to get into the mystery of the Eucharistic Prayer.

For prayer and discussion

• Have you noticed the "change of tone" when we get to the Preface? It gives us something to praise God for that "lifts up our hearts" in wonder at what God has done for us. Do you pick up a new note of excitement?

• When we make the responses back and forth with the presider at the beginning of the Preface, do you feel you are at a pep rally? What is the same and what is different?

• When you sing the *Sanctus* ("Holy, holy, holy"), do you feel yourself surrounded by angels and saints? Do you feel part of their chorus?

• Do you think that a fresh look at the Preface might help you to get "out of this world" during Mass? What have you realized in reading this that might help you do that?

CHAPTER SIXTEEN

The Eucharistic Prayer
We Are Priest
and Victim

The church calls the Eucharistic Prayer "the center and high point of the entire celebration" of Mass (*General Instruction of the Roman Missal*, no. 78). To enter into it—and participate in its action—is the real reason why Catholics go to Mass. There are plenty of other reasons—good reasons, worthwhile reasons—but none is on the level of this one. We assemble to praise and thank God, to pray for ourselves and the world, to give and find support for our faith in community, to hear the word of God and recommit ourselves to living it, to experience the "peace and unity" of communion with each other in communion with the Father, Son, and Spirit. Any one of these is a sufficient reason for attending church on Sunday. But none comes close to the reason we find in "the center and summit of the entire celebration," the Eucharistic Prayer.

What is the mystery and meaning of the Eucharistic Prayer?

When we begin the Eucharistic Prayer we enter most fully

into that real world whose history revolves around the crucifixion and resurrection of Jesus. If we are not conscious that the cross of Jesus is at the center of time—in the sense that it gives meaning and value to everything else, and that we need to see everything else in relationship to what took place on the cross— we understand nothing about the world we live in or about ourselves as existing in it. For us, reality is what Saint Paul describes:

> God has rescued us from the power of darkness and transferred us into the kingdom of his beloved Son, in whom we have redemption, the forgiveness of sins.
>
> He is the image of the invisible God, the firstborn of all creation. He is the head of the body, the church; he is the beginning, the firstborn from the dead, so that he might come to have first place in everything. For in him all the fullness of God was pleased to dwell, and through him God was pleased to reconcile to himself all things, whether on earth or in heaven, by making peace through the blood of his cross. (COLOSSIANS 1:13–20)

This, Paul says, is "the mystery that has been hidden throughout the ages and generations but has now been revealed to his saints." This is what we celebrate in the "real world" of the Eucharistic Prayer at Mass. Any culture that denies this mystery, ignores it, or is just unaware of it is a society of people "sitting in darkness and in the shadow of death" (Matthew 4:16; Luke 1:79). But the truth is, this mystery is ignored in the "ordinary" world of daily life. That world is a shadow world of ignorance. The Mass takes us out of that world and "into his marvelous light" (1 Peter 2:9).

The central mystery and moment of the Mass is simply this: during the Eucharistic Prayer we consciously join ourselves to

Jesus Christ offering himself—and offering us with and in himself as members of his body on the cross—for the life of the world.

We don't gather just to watch Jesus offering himself for us. Or to adore him while he is doing it. Much less do we gather to watch the ordained priest offer him in our name. The mystery and true meaning of the Eucharistic Prayer is not that Christ dies *for* us, but that we die *with* and *in* him.

Jesus as "Lamb of God" does not "take away the sins of the world" by "paying the price" for our sins as if he were taking some kind of punishment for us. The "price" Jesus paid was to "redeem" us ("buy us back") out of slavery (1 Corinthians 6:20; 7:23). If God did require "satisfaction" or "punishment" for sin (which is a common teaching in the church, but is not something the church teaches as divine revelation), the acceptance of that punishment by Jesus would not take away our sins. Someone else taking punishment for us does not change us at all, any more than another's act of forgiving changes anything in us. Sins can only be "taken away" when our history comes to an end in death. And then it can happen only if we ourselves change by rising again with Christ and in Christ as a "new creation," which is the phrase Saint Paul uses to describe the baptized. So the death of Christ is redemptive for us *only because we are included in it.* We participated in it. It was our death. This is the way Saint Paul explains baptism:

> Do you not know that all of us who have been baptized
> into Christ Jesus were baptized into his death? Therefore
> we have been buried with him by baptism into death, so
> that, just as Christ was raised from the dead by the glory
> of the Father, so we too might walk in newness of life. For
> if we have been united with him in a death like his, we will

certainly be united with him in a resurrection like his. We
know that our old self was crucified with him so that the
body of sin might be destroyed, and we might no longer be
enslaved to sin. For whoever has died is freed from sin. But
if we have died with Christ, we believe that we will also live
with him. (ROMANS 6:3–8)

This means that what we are called to do at Mass during the
Eucharistic Prayer is to *join in the action* that is taking place
on the altar when Jesus, offering himself on Calvary, becomes
present in our time and place. When his body hung on the cross,
we were in that body, having been incorporated into it, with all
of our sins, by baptism. When Jesus as Priest offered himself as
Victim, his "flesh for the life of the world," we were in the body
that was offered. Now, at Mass, knowing by the light of faith the
mystery that is taking place, and being present to it—as truly as
Mary and others at the foot of the cross were present to it two
thousand years ago—we are called, as "priests in the Priest," to
offer ourselves intensely with Christ and in Christ now as "victims in the Victim"—our own "flesh for the life of the world."

It is this mystery taking place that makes the Eucharistic
Prayer "the center and high point of the entire celebration" of
Mass. Therefore, to participate in Eucharist as we should, the
one most important thing we need to do (although "full, active, conscious participation" in every part of the celebration is
called for) is *join in the action* and offer ourselves as members
of the body of Christ, "through him, and with him, and in him"
during the Eucharistic Prayer. We do this most intensely during
the institution narrative when the presider repeats the words
of Jesus—"This is my Body...given up for you...the cup of my
Blood...poured out for you..."—and follows up the words by

showing Christ's Body and Blood to the assembly.

When the presider lifts up the host, we are in that host, just as we were in the body of Christ that was lifted up on the cross. When we see Christ, and ourselves in Christ, lifted up at Mass, we need to be repeating in our hearts the words that describe the action: "*This is my body, given up for you.*" We need to focus on the action: Christ's action and ours.

Probably the greatest deviation of Catholic devotion during the Eucharistic Prayer is a misguided practice that is taking on renewed popularity in our time. It is the error of turning the "elevation" after the institution narrative into an act of adoration instead of focusing on the action of offering ourselves with and in Jesus. Adoration is good. But if it distracts us from participating in the action of the Mass, then it is an aberration.

The French bishops may have made this mistake in the ninth century when they decided to convert the Mass into a teaching instrument to combat the Arian heresy, which downplayed the divinity of Christ. They introduced changes into the liturgy that promoted adoration rather than active participation. Their intention was good, but the changes stressed the awesomeness and distance of God in such a way that the laity were made to feel unworthy of taking an active part in the sacred ceremony of the Mass, which was no longer recognized as a communal celebration. Bishop Patrick Dunn describes the results:

> A ritual confession of sinfulness was added to the introductory rite, and the priests genuflected in adoration after the consecration. The canon [Eucharistic Prayer] was whispered—to protect and honor the mystery. The laity were discouraged from receiving communion too frequently, and certainly not with their hands! The Creed of

Nicaea [with the words "consubstantial with the Father"] was inserted between the Gospel and the Canon. The priest often prayed now with his hands joined in supplication, rather than outstretched in thanksgiving. Because the Mass was seen primarily as a sacrifice, the sermon seemed to be increasingly superfluous...

These changes were also reflected in architecture. As early as the fourth century the notion that the priest "led" the people to God meant that altars were placed against the rear wall. This allowed the people to stand "behind" their leader, rather than "around" the altar for a sacrifice which they "all" offered. The people now "watched," and from an increasing distance, separated firstly by monastic stalls, then by ornate sanctuary screens, and then by communion rails at which people could kneel. With the discovery of the pointed arch, cathedrals became even more spacious, and the people more distant.

The liturgy, which had once been a communal prayer, was now a clerical ritual, isolated by distance and language [Latin, mysterious and unintelligible to the people]. Instead of casting light on the Christian mysteries, the liturgy itself had become a mystery! (*Priesthood: A Re-Examination of the Roman Catholic Theology of the Presbyterate* [Alba House, New York, 1990], pages 81-85)

Most of these changes are still embodied in the liturgy. And despite the efforts since Vatican II, they are still producing the same effect. A large number of people come to Mass to kneel silently in the pews. When the climactic moment of the Eucharistic

Prayer comes—when Jesus' Body and Blood are presented to us in the very act of his sacrifice—these people are often so focused on adoration that they miss the liturgy's invitation to offer themselves with and in Jesus. When they should be echoing his words and declaring in their hearts, "This is my body, offered for you" (for every person in the world), they gaze in motionless adoration instead and simply reaffirm their faith: "My Lord and my God!"

Saint Ignatius of Loyola's teaching on spiritual discernment warns us against accepting, not only what is "evil," or what is "distracting," but also anything that is "less good than what we had originally proposed to do" (*Spiritual Exercises*, 333). We are misled when we do something good at Mass (like praying the rosary, or turning the Mass into eucharistic adoration) instead of participating fully, consciously, and actively in the mystery that is actually taking place. Adoration is good, and it certainly has its place. But, in the context of Mass, if it is less good than what the church had originally proposed for us to do, it is not what God is asking us to do at this time.

If we take a fresh look at the Mass and begin to listen attentively to all the words of the Eucharistic Prayer, we will begin to appreciate the *mystery* of the Mass—that which "invites endless exploration."

We will never be bored again.

ARE YOU A "HEARER" OR A "DOER"?

It helps little to take a "fresh look" at the Mass if what we see does not change what we do. Saint James said:

> Be doers of the word, and not merely hearers who deceive

themselves. For if any are hearers of the word and not doers, they are like those who look at themselves in a mirror;
for they look at themselves and, on going away, immedi-
ately forget what they were like. But those who look into
the perfect law, the law of liberty, and persevere, being not
hearers who forget but doers who act—they will be blessed
in their doing. (**JAMES 1:22–25**)

So if you are going to offer yourself—consciously, actively, fully—with Christ when the host is lifted up at Mass, that involves
three things:

1. *A fresh acceptance of the mystery of your new identity*: At baptism you "became Christ." It is only because of that mystery that
you can see yourself in the host and join yourself to Christ offering his body at Mass for the life of the world. So you may have
to "convert" to real belief that you are the living body of Jesus
on earth, that "*through him, and with him,* and *in him,*" you are
saving the world, and that he acts *with you, in you,* and *through
you* to give life to others in everything you do. You can believe
that or not, but as we proclaim in the *Rite of Baptism*: "This is our
faith. This is the faith of the Church. We are proud to profess it,
in Christ Jesus our Lord." (See also the *Catechism of the Catholic
Church*, no. 795.)

Offering yourself consciously with and in Jesus at Mass will
help you grow into the mystical experience of knowing you have
become Christ. Go for it!

2. *A fresh understanding and acceptance of your baptismal
anointing as "priest"*: The words of your anointing with chrism
at baptism were: "As Christ was anointed *Priest, Prophet and*

King, so live always as a member of his body."

So you are a priest. That is not a choice any longer; it is a fact. Your only choice is whether to live out your baptismal anointing as priest and live up to it, or be an "unfaithful servant." What do you choose to do?

Offering Christ at Mass, and yourself in him, will help you grow into understanding yourself as a "priest in the Priest" and "victim in the Victim." Then you can grow into living out this sacrifice all day, every day.

3. *A fresh commitment to bring the offering of yourself down to earth in daily life*: In concrete practice, to offer, in Christ, your "flesh for the life of the world" is very simple. In every encounter with another person—in family, business, or social life—you "present your body as a living sacrifice to God," as you did at baptism. This means that in every human interaction you are "sacrificed" to letting Jesus Christ act *with you, in you*, and *through you* to give or enhance God's divine life in others. In dealing with every other person, like Saint Paul, you are "in the pain of childbirth until Christ is formed" in them. By accepting baptism, you accepted, as an inseparable part of it, the "work of ministry, for building up the body of Christ until all of us come to the unity of the faith and of the knowledge of the Son of God, to maturity, to the measure of the full stature of Christ." That is your job description as *priest* (see Galatians 4:19; Ephesians 4:12–13).

How do you do this? It is simple. *Express yourself.*

Your real self, of course. Not the self you are perceived to be in the unreal world of the culture, but the self you proclaim yourself to be at Mass: your divine self. To be "priest in the Priest," just let the invisible life of grace in you (God's life) become visible in your physical words and actions. Let your flesh be the medium for God's expression of truth (your faith), for God's promise of fulfillment (your hope), and for God's constant manifestation of love (your love made flesh in action).

Smile at strangers. Treat everyone as you would treat your brother or sister, because our faith tells us we are all called to be brothers and sisters in Christ. If you see something good in another person, say it. Praise and thank people constantly.

Paul taught, "The gifts God gave were that some would be apostles, some prophets, some evangelists, some pastors and teachers, to equip the saints for the work of ministry, for building up the body of Christ" (Ephesians 4:11–12). We recognize that, in the same way, God gifted some to be janitors, some to be managers, some corporate executives or waitresses—but all of them equally "for the work of ministry, for building up the body of Christ." So we praise and thank them all. We compliment the janitor for the way he mops the floor, and the waitress for her attention, as much as we compliment the manager for kindness shown to an employee or the president of the company for good decisions. We know "there are varieties of gifts, but the same Spirit; and there are varieties of services, but the same Lord; and there are varieties of activities, but it is the same God who activates all of them in everyone" (1 Corinthians 12:4–6). We praise and thank God for them all. And we are not embarrassed to do it out loud. To do this is to give flesh to the words of faith.

When things are tough, Saint Peter tells us, "Do not fear... and do not be intimidated." Don't hide your light under a basket. Show the confidence, the peace, that comes from faith. "If you are asked about your Christian hope, always be ready to explain it" (1 Peter 3:14–15). Let what is inside of you show outside. Let your divine life take flesh in your human words and actions. That is what it means to be a "priest in the Priest."

It will make you also a "victim in the Victim." It costs to express yourself. Exposing yourself—especially your divine self—to others makes you vulnerable. To do this is to "die to self." But Jesus said there is "no greater love than this, to lay down one's life for one's friends" (John 15:13). To "offer your body as a living sacrifice" by giving physical expression to your faith, hope, and love is to give your "flesh for the life of the world."

For prayer and discussion

• What do you usually do when the Body and Blood of Christ are lifted up during the Eucharistic Prayer?

• Do you think this moment is especially sacred because that is when the bread and wine are changed into Christ's Body and Blood? Or because that is when his act of offering himself on the cross is made present?

• If you focus on adoring Jesus when the host and chalice are lifted up, how will that affect your conduct after Mass? If you focus on joining yourself to the action of offering your body with his for the life of the world, how will that affect your behavior after Mass?

• Give some concrete examples of how you can "offer your body as a living sacrifice" for others on the ground level of daily life?

The Rite of Communion

To Feel and Fashion the Future

The Mass ends with a foretaste of heaven. As soon as the Communion Rite begins (with the Our Father) we are in the "end time," the time of Christ's total victory over sin and death, when the whole redeemed human race will be together in perfect peace and unity.

Pope Francis proclaimed this reality in *The Joy of the Gospel* (no. 229):

> Christ has made all things one in himself: heaven and earth, God and humanity, time and eternity, flesh and spirit, person and society. The sign of this unity and reconciliation of all things in him is peace. Christ "is our peace" (Ephesians 2:14)…Peace is possible because the Lord has overcome the world and its constant conflict "by making peace through the blood of his cross" (Colossians 1:20).

The real world that we experience during liturgy we experience in a special way during the Communion Rite, which is and is meant to be a preview, an experience beforehand, of the peace and "blessed hope" we are actively awaiting: the "manifestation of the glory of our great God and Savior, Jesus Christ" (Titus 2:13).

During the Communion Rite we are present—in fact and not in fantasy—at the "wedding banquet of the Lamb." That "Lamb," of course, is Jesus, the "Lamb of God." The Book of Revelation shows him as victorious at the end of time:

> I looked, and I heard the voice of many angels surrounding the throne and the living creatures and the elders; they numbered myriads of myriads and thousands of thousands, singing with full voice, "Worthy is the Lamb that was slaughtered to receive power and wealth and wisdom and might and honor and glory and blessing!" Then I heard every creature in heaven and on earth and under the earth and in the sea, and all that is in them, singing, "To the one seated on the throne and to the Lamb be blessing and honor and glory and might forever and ever!" (REVELATION 5:11–13)

Jesus described heaven as a banquet. The Book of Revelation, recognizing that the church is the bride of Christ, calls it the "wedding banquet of the Lamb."

> Then I heard what seemed to be the voice of a great multitude, like the sound of many waters and like the sound of mighty thunderpeals, crying out, "Hallelujah! For the Lord our God the Almighty reigns. Let us rejoice and exult and

give him the glory, for the marriage of the Lamb has come,
and his bride has made herself ready; to her it has been
granted to be clothed with fine linen, bright and pure"—
for the fine linen is the righteous deeds of the saints. And
the angel said to me, "Write this: Blessed are those who are
invited to the marriage supper of the Lamb." (REVELATION
19:6–9)

In the timeframe of God, in which everything is one eternal
"now," the world has already come to an end. Christ is reigning
in triumph. The Lamb of God has taken away the sins of the
world. Death holds no menace for us. The wedding banquet is
already going on. When we die, we are simply propelled into the
party. "Happy are those who are invited to the marriage supper
of the Lamb."

At Eucharist we are already there. The Communion Rite is its
preview. Receiving communion gives us a taste of it. However,
in our earthly, provisional timeframe of before and after, this
moment has not yet arrived. We are still in the world we live in.
But it is an ephemeral world, nothing but a "staging area," a time
and place as transient as childhood. To perceive as permanent a
world that, in the whole view of things, has already disappeared
would be as foolish as playing obliviously in a rain puddle, thinking it is the fountain of youth. The Communion Rite takes us out
of this illusion.

The essential reality of communion is the real presence of
Jesus—of his living sacramental body—individually in each one
of us, and communally in all of us together. We are one with him
and with each other as we will be in heaven. For the few brief
moments when we are all together after communion, united in
the common experience of having received Jesus into our bod-

ies and souls, nothing divides us. We are not fighting. We are not taking advantage of one another. We are not even harboring resentments, although they may come flooding back into our consciousness when Mass is over. During communion we are conscious only of the "peace and unity" of his kingdom. It is a preview of the "wedding banquet of the Lamb."

Let's look at the steps that lead up to this.

THE LORD'S PRAYER

We begin the Communion Rite when the presider invites us to "pray with confidence to the Father in the words our Savior gave us." And we pray the Our Father together. All the petitions of the Our Father are asking for the *Parousia*—the second coming of Jesus in triumph and glory. We will celebrate and experience his triumph in the "wedding banquet of the Lamb." When all are gathered together, celebrating the marriage of Jesus and his church, everything we ask for now in the Lord's Prayer we will experience then as an accomplished fact.

At the wedding banquet we will see that:

The Father is known and loved, his name "hallowed," by the whole human race.

His kingdom has come. His will is being done on earth as it is in heaven.

He is giving us "this day" the "bread of tomorrow"—Jesus, Bread of Life, joy of the wedding feast.

We are all forgiving one another as we are being forgiven by God. To eat of this Bread we must sit down together with others in peace and unity. The Bread of heaven is served in a communal meal. This presupposes total mutual forgiveness.

THE SIGN OF PEACE

The most frequently used word in the Communion Rite is "peace." "Grant us peace in our day." "Peace I leave you, my peace I give you." "Grant us the peace and unity" that are according to your heart. "The peace of the Lord be with you always." "Let us offer each other the sign of peace."

The Sign of Peace is an "eschatological" sign—that is, something that points to the "end time," when Christ's victory is complete. When we embrace or shake hands with each other before communion, we are not saying all is well between us. In some cases, that could be hypocrisy. No, we are saying we *believe*, and we *desire*, that at the "wedding banquet of the Lamb," all will be well between us. Forgiveness is not always reconciliation, and only complete reconciliation brings peace. We are saying that we want complete reconciliation with everyone, both on this earth and in heaven, here and now and forever. We are open to it. And what we cannot bring about by ourselves at this moment, we ask the "Lamb of God" to bring about, knowing he will. He *takes away* the sins of the world." We pray to him with confidence: "*Grant us peace.*"

THE BREAKING OF THE BREAD

As the whole assembly chants the triple "Lamb of God," the presider breaks the bread, just as Jesus—when he fed the multitude with just a few loaves of bread—"looked up to heaven, blessed and broke them, and gave them to the disciples to set before the crowd" (Luke 9:16). Luke and other Scripture writers keep the formula intact: "*blessed, broke, gave*" (see Luke 22:19, 24:30; 1

Corinthians 11:23–24). Eucharist is many grains of wheat that "die" to become one bread: a bread that is broken to be shared with many. Eucharist is the *"sacrament of unity* in the Church," a symbol of unity that produces the unity it symbolizes. (See Henri de Lubac, SJ, *Catholicism* [Burns and Oates, 1950], pp. 35 ff.)

This unity is a *mystery*. It is the mystery expressed in the many grains of wheat ground into flour that calls us to give up our self-enclosed individuality to be made one bread. The many grapes, crushed, mingled, and poured together, are "lost and found again" as one wine. It is the mystery of Jesus Christ, the seed who "fell into the ground and died" so that "all might be made one" as members of his body risen from the grave.

THE THIRD "ELEVATION"

There are three "elevations" in the Mass, and they are reminiscent of our former Memorial Acclamation: *"Christ has died, Christ is risen, Christ will come again."*

The first is after the words "This is my body...the cup of my Blood..." which will be "given up...poured out for you." At this time the presider is instructed to "show" (not lift aloft for adoration) the consecrated host, and afterwards the chalice, to the people. The focus is on "Christ has died." The Body and Blood of Christ are shown separated as in death. We are called to offer ourselves with and in Jesus on the cross.

The second "elevation" is at the end of the Eucharistic Prayer, when the presider is told to pick up together the chalice and the host. The Body and Blood are reunited as in resurrection, and the presider "raises" them to proclaim that if we, who are the risen body of Christ on earth, act "through him, and with him, and in him" as one united church, "in the unity of the Holy Spirit," then it will be seen that "all glory and honor is yours, almighty

Father, forever and ever." Now the focus is on "Christ has risen." We are called to live as Christ's risen and united body on earth.

The third "elevation" is in the Communion Rite, when the presider is instructed, while facing the people, to hold the host "slightly raised above the paten or chalice," while saying: "Behold the Lamb of God, behold him who takes away the sins of the world. Blessed are those who are called to the marriage supper of the Lamb."*

[* *The liturgical text omits the word "marriage" from this otherwise word-for-word repetition of verse 9, chapter 19, of St. Jerome's Latin translation of the Book of Revelation. This was probably due to a sleepy copyist's error centuries ago that no one noticed until the words were fixed in the immutability of the status quo. The American bishops were informed of the error before the new translation of 2011 but voted to continue it rather than depart from strict adherence to the Latin liturgical text.*]

One real meaning of this proclamation is, "Blessed are those who are going to die!" This is the church's triumphant shout in the face of every threat, every persecution, even death itself: "Happy are those who are going to die!" Nothing can harm us. Jesus the victorious Lamb of God has conquered sin and death. He has "taken away the sins of the world. Blessed are those who are called to the wedding banquet of the Lamb!" Death simply opens the door to the party and pushes us in.

Now the focus is on "Christ will come again!" We are called, as faithful stewards of his kingship, to persevere in working to establish his reign over every area and activity of human life on earth until he returns in triumph. This will arouse the world against us. But Jesus said, "In me you have peace. In the world you face persecution. But take courage; I have overcome the world!" (John 16:33).

THE DISTRIBUTION OF COMMUNION

Now we approach the altar to receive the Bread of Life. We have come a long way. Gone are the days when a distorted emphasis on the majesty of God told us we were unworthy to receive communion more than once a year—or monthly at most. Gone is the misguided clericalism that forbade the laity to touch the Body of Christ with their hands, although their hands were the hands of Christ. Only the anointed hands of the ordained priest were considered worthy to touch the sacred host. Even Mary, the Mother of God, would not have been allowed to take the sacramental Body of Christ into the hands that held him as a baby.

Now it is different. Now, instead of training us to approach communion like mourners going up to a casket, in silence, heads bowed, intent only on Jesus and oblivious of everyone else, the church tells us communion is supposed to look and feel as much as possible like a family meal.

Now the church tells us to sing while we go up to communion. In some countries the people dance up. The purpose of singing—or dancing—is "to express the spiritual union of the communicants by means of the unity of their voices, to show gladness of heart, and to bring out more clearly the 'communitarian' character of the procession to receive the Eucharist" (*General Instruction of the Roman Missal*, 86).

We should look around. Watch everyone being fed. See Jesus giving himself to people we didn't think were that important. But Jesus is happy to "enter under their roof." This changes our perspective, like seeing the president's limo pulling up before the house of our next-door neighbor. Communion should make us appreciate each other more.

For this, it helps to look around and see people approaching the table. Prayer does not always require us to close our eyes. How can we appreciate the mystery of sharing in the life of God—whose life is *relationship*: the interaction of Father, Son, and Spirit—if our only experience of "prayer" is isolationist individualism?

There is a time to be "alone with Jesus." It is after all have received. The *Instruction* says, "When the distribution of Communion is finished," all should "pray quietly for some time."

This is the time to enclose ourselves with Jesus, to acknowledge his presence in our hearts. We don't need to speak words or meditate. We just need to be aware that he is in us and that we are with him. This is a preview of heaven.

We have not separated ourselves from the rest of the assembly. We know we are sharing this moment of intimacy with Christ together. We are all united with him. And "in him" we are united to each other. In communion we experience most deeply that "communion of the Holy Spirit" proclaimed at the beginning of Mass.

We know that we are about to go out into the unreal world again. We know that outside there is division, disunity, and violence. But for the moment, we put all else aside and rest in the presence and possession of Christ, surrendered in body, mind, and soul to the "peace and unity" of his kingdom. We experience it. We feel it.

And because we do, we are motivated to work, when we go out again, to establish the "peace and unity" of his kingdom throughout the world. The peace we enjoy is not a peace for us alone. It is a "preview peace." It is a sample of what we are sent to establish in every area of our stewardship: at home and at work; at school and in our social circles. We are called to work for change. To right what is wrong in politics and in religion. To call for the truth in church and in government, in business policies and church practices.

All is not well on earth. But Christ has won the victory. And for a few fleeting moments we have felt the peace and unity of his kingdom, where

> the wolf shall lie with the lamb, and the leopard
>   with the newborn kid...
> the lion shall eat straw like the ox....
> And they will not hurt or destroy on all my holy mountain.
> For the earth will be full of the knowledge of the LORD
> As the waters cover the sea. (ISAIAH 11:6–9)

This is the experience, this is the foretaste, that motivates us to go out from Mass and abandon ourselves in working for the kingdom of God. Having experienced for a moment what is and what can be, we are then "sent forth" with renewed motivation, as "stewards of the kingship of Christ," to take responsibility— and exercise leadership—in making it happen.

For prayer and discussion

- In communion, are you more focused on Jesus coming to you individually, or on Jesus giving himself to everyone together?

- Do you make yourself aware that communion is a foretaste of heaven? Do you ever experience a quiet, a peace, that makes you think, "If I died right now, it would be okay"?

- Are you conscious during communion that one day the whole human race will be united in the "peace and unity" of this moment?

- Does the "victory" you experience in preview give you hope, confidence, and motivation to go out and work to establish this peace throughout the world?

CHAPTER EIGHTEEN

"Go forth, the Mass is ended"

To Live and Give the Good News

The Rite of Dismissal at Mass—"Go forth, the Mass is ended"—echoes the last words Jesus spoke on earth, the words of the "Great Commission":

> All authority in heaven and on earth has been given to me. Go therefore and make disciples of all nations, baptizing them in the name of the Father and of the Son and of the Holy Spirit, and teaching them to obey everything that I have commanded you. And remember, I am with you always, to the end of the age. (**MATTHEW 28:18–20**)

"Go forth as disciples. Learn, share, make disciples of all you meet."

"Go forth as prophets, to live and give the Good News. Bear witness to me by your lifestyle."

"Go forth as priests; find and nurture my sheep."

"Go forth in peace, as stewards of my kingship, to bring my peace to the world."

"Go forth as my body. Let me work *with you, in you,* and *through you* in all you do."

We go forth from the real world celebrated at Mass to bring the unreal world into the "peace and unity" of his kingdom.

The Eucharist ends as it began, with a call to bring the world into *relationship* with the Three Persons of the Trinity. We began "In the name of the Father, and of the Son, and of the Holy Spirit." We end with a final blessing: "May almighty God bless you, the Father, and the Son, and the Holy Spirit." We go out as sent to baptize the world "in the name of the Father, and of the Son, and of the Holy Spirit."

God is relationship. Relationship is interaction. Eucharist is an invitation to interact with God and with others until Christ's prayer is realized: "I ask…that they may all be one. As you, Father, are in me and I am in you, may they also be in us, so that the world may believe that you have sent me" (John 17:20–21).

Go forth! To live and give the Good News!

For prayer and discussion

- When you leave church after Mass, do you feel that something has ended or is just beginning?

- When you left church after your wedding, how did you feel then? Do you see a similarity?

- How do you share with others what you have received at Mass?

CHAPTER NINETEEN

The "Source and Summit"
Starting Point and High Point of our Week

T he bishops proclaimed in the Second Vatican Council that the celebration of Eucharist is the "source and summit of the Christian life." Mass should be—and can be—the starting point and high point of our week, and of our lives as Christians.

The explanation of that statement lies in two sentences:

The most important thing Jesus did in his life was to let us share in his death.

Mass is a mystery of memory made present.

THE SOURCE

Our Christian life begins at baptism. The essence of baptism is incorporation into the dying and rising of Jesus. We are "baptized into his death." By baptism we died with him and rose in him: rose as a "new creation," as his body, to let Jesus the Messiah continue to live his life and fulfill his mission *with us, in us,* and *through us* until he comes again. Baptism is union with Jesus in his death and resurrection.

The celebration of Eucharist makes this mystery present. The mystery of the Mass is that it does not *repeat* the sacrifice of Calvary but *makes it present* in our time and space. Through remembrance.

To "celebrate" is to "single out for grateful remembrance."

> Jesus took a loaf of bread, and when he had given thanks, he broke it and gave it to them, saying, "This is my body, which is given for you. Do this in remembrance of me."
> (LUKE 22:19)
> In the same way he took the cup also, after supper, saying, "This cup is the new covenant in my blood. Do this, as often as you drink it, in remembrance of me."
> (1 CORINTHIANS 11:25)

At Mass, what we remember is really present. Eucharist is a sacrament. A sacrament is an action of God that takes place through human words and actions. In a sacrament, what is expressed in symbol is accomplished in reality. In the sacrament of the Mass, the eucharistic remembrance makes really present what is remembered in words and reenacted in symbol. So during Mass, the death and rising of Jesus, which took place two thousand years ago outside of Jerusalem, becomes really present on the altar when and where we celebrate it. Making that memory present is what keeps our faith, hope, and love alive.

In the Mass as "source," there are five things the Mass reminds us to keep in mind all week:

1. Cultivating awareness

The first "building block" of spiritual growth is to *cultivate awareness* of the *new identity* we have through baptism. This identity is a *relationship* we are constantly growing into through conscious *interaction* with the Father, Son, and Spirit. The Introductory Rites of the Mass immerse us in this awareness with gratitude and praise. They remind us to cultivate this awareness all week.

2. Commitment to discipleship

The second building block of our spiritual growth is a commitment to *discipleship*—that is, to being "students" of the mind and heart of Christ by reflecting on his words. Once we accept that we have "become Christ" by baptism, the next logical step is to learn how to think and act like Jesus. This leads us to the "three Rs" of scriptural prayer: to *read, reflect,* and *respond* to Christ's self-revelation in the gospel.

This is the declared purpose of the second phase of the Mass: to start us meditating on the Scriptures and sustain us in it: "The Liturgy of the Word is to be celebrated in such a way as to *favor meditation*, in which, by the prompting of the Holy Spirit, the Word of God may be grasped by the heart and a response [of the will] through prayer may be prepared" (*General Instruction of the Roman Missal*, no. 56).

The source of our Christian growth as disciples is repeated encounter with the living Jesus, teaching us through his word. We refresh this encounter every week during Eucharist. Ideally, we reflect on the Scripture readings and share the fruit of our reflection in discussion with others. Then we experience the living Jesus giving light to us all, both individually and communally, in the "communion of the Holy Spirit." This is to let Eucharist continue to form us as "many grains of wheat" united as one bread, which is what it means to be "church."

3. Dedication to mission

The third building block of spiritual growth is *dedication* to the *mission* of Jesus. We were consecrated to this at baptism when we were anointed to share in Christ's messianic mission as priest, prophet, and king. Our first conscious acceptance of this mission typically takes place when we dedicate ourselves to bearing *witness* to the Good News as *prophets.* In practice, this means living a lifestyle that cannot be explained unless we are enlightened by God's word and empowered by his Holy Spirit.

At Mass, the message of the Presentation of Gifts is that God uses created things and persons—the "fruit of the earth and the work of human hands"—to produce divine effects. When we intentionally put ourselves on the altar under the symbols of bread and wine, we are "presenting our bodies as a living sacrifice" to be used for God's divine work. We do this, first of all, by living in a way that cannot be explained without grace. This means we live by the New Law of the Sermon on the Mount instead of by the good but earlier standards of the Ten Commandments. To do this is to dedicate ourselves to bearing witness to the values of Jesus in all our words, choices, and actions.

If we consciously renew this dedication in every Mass during the Presentation of Gifts, the Eucharist becomes the source and support of our dedication as "prophets," which is the third phase of Christian spiritual growth.

4. Surrender to ministry

The fourth building block of spiritual growth is *surrender* to letting Jesus express himself in us and through us to others in *ministry*. This is to live out our baptismal consecration as *priests*.

Ministry is included, of course, in the messianic mission of Jesus as priest, prophet, and king. But there is a nuance of difference. "Mission" suggests dedication to a cause, such as announcing the Good News to the whole world. "Ministry" suggests nurturing and caring for people. It has a more gentle and personal tone.

Also, "mission" evokes an image of power, even though it is empowerment by the Holy Spirit. In "ministry" there is no power except in a mutual experience of Jesus present and acting in his nurturing body. That is what heals. That is what gives divine life. That is what brings divine life to fullness in those to whom we minister.

That is why ministry consists essentially in *surrender* to Jesus expressing his love to others *with us, in us,* and *through us.* To surrender to this—that is, to Jesus doing this in us—in every encounter, with every person we deal with, is the fourth phase of growth into the fullness of Christian life

This surrender is embodied and renewed in the Eucharistic Prayer at Mass.

When the presider lifts up the host to show it to the congregation after the institution narrative at Mass, we repeat, we echo in our hearts, the words of that narrative: "This is *my* body, given up for *you*." This is a pledge, a commitment to "offer our bodies" as "priests in the Priest" and "victims in the Victim" to let Jesus continue to express himself to others in and through our physical words and actions. This is to offer our "flesh for the life of the world."

In practice, this means we overcome our resistance to self-exposure. We embrace the vulnerability of giving physical expression to our faith, hope, and love in words and actions that reveal the loving presence of Jesus within us. To surrender ourselves to this—and renew that surrender at every Mass—is to enter into the fourth phase of spiritual growth, which is to surrender to letting Jesus express himself in us and through us to others in ministry. The mystery of the offering we make of Jesus and of ourselves—*through him, with him, and in him*—is what makes the Eucharistic Prayer "the center and summit of the entire celebration" of Mass. And this, more than anything else, is what makes Eucharist the "source and summit of the Christian life."

5. Abandonment to stewardship

Beyond surrender there is total *abandonment*. This is the fifth and final phase of spiritual growth.

Surrender can take place in multiple, repeated acts. But abandonment is the once-and-for-all gift of all that one has and is, never to be retracted or repeated. It can be renewed, of course, and ideally should be during the Rite of Communion in every Mass. This is the full acceptance of our baptismal anointing as kings or stewards of the kingship of Christ.

Stewardship is the acceptance of responsibility for managing what belongs to another. Christian stewardship consists, first of all, in returning to God all he has given us, and then—since he puts it all back in our hands—in taking responsibility for managing everything we have, or have control over, in the way that best contributes to the establishment of the reign of God on earth.

What is asked of stewards is *fidelity*, which is faith preserved in practice. To be "faithful stewards" of the kingship of Christ, we need to *persevere* in working for the establishment of his kingdom until he comes again. We sustain perseverance by looking forward with hope to the "end time" when Christ will return in triumph and glory. This is the fifth building block in the structure of the Christian life.

> Sell your possessions, and give alms. Make purses for yourselves that do not wear out, an unfailing treasure in heaven...For where your treasure is, there your heart will be also.
>
> Be dressed for action and have your lamps lit; be like those who are waiting for their master to return from the wedding banquet, so that they may open the door for him as soon as he comes and knocks. Blessed are those servants whom the master finds alert when he comes; truly I tell you, he will fasten his belt and have them sit down to eat, and he will come and serve them...
>
> Who then is the faithful and prudent steward whom his master will put in charge of his servants, to give them their allowance of food at the proper time? Blessed is that servant whom his master will find at work when he arrives. Truly I tell you, he will put that one in charge of all his possessions. (LUKE 12:33–37, 42–44)

In the Communion Rite at Mass, we celebrate in preview Christ's return at the end of time. In communion, Jesus literally has us "sit down to eat," and he "comes and serves us." It is a preview of the "wedding banquet of the Lamb," where all of redeemed humanity, united by the Holy Spirit, are seated together at the table of their Father in total reconciliation and mutual love.

This is, and is meant to be, motivating.

Receiving communion at Mass is the strongest source of perseverance in the Christian life, especially in the total abandonment of stewardship.

> The angel of the LORD came to Elijah, touched him, and said, "Get up and eat, otherwise the journey will be too much for you." He got up, and ate and drank; then he went in the strength of that food forty days and forty nights to Horeb the mount of God. (1 KINGS 19:7–8)

> Then Jesus called his disciples to him and said, "I have compassion for the crowd, because they have been with me now for three days and have nothing to eat; and I do not want to send them away hungry, for they might faint on the way."
>
> Then ordering the crowd to sit down on the ground, he took the seven loaves and the fish; and after giving thanks he broke them and gave them to the disciples, and the disciples gave them to the crowds. And all of them ate and were filled; and they took up the broken pieces left over, seven baskets full. (MATTHEW 15:32, 35–37)

In stewardship, we make the gift of all for All. In communion we receive the gift of All for all. In all the other sacraments, Jesus comes to do some particular thing for us. In Eucharist he simply gives us himself. As he will in heaven.

And we simply give him ourselves, all that we are, as we will be totally given in heaven.

> Take, Lord, and receive all my liberty, my memory, my understanding, and my entire will—all that I have and

possess. You have given all to me. To you, Lord, I return it. All is yours. Dispose of it wholly according to your will. Give me your love and your grace. That is enough for me. (St. Ignatius of Loyola, *The Spiritual Exercises*, 234. Based on the translation by George Ganss, SJ, Loyola University Press, 1992.)

This is stewardship brought to total abandonment. It is the fifth and final phase of our growth as Christians to the "perfection of love." We find its source and summit in Communion.

Stop...and Go

Jesus pinned his hope on the Mass to keep his followers together: to keep his words alive among us and keep our hearts on fire. For the Mass to do this, all we have to do is *pay attention* while at Mass, understand what we are paying attention to, and *participate* fully, actively, and consciously.

Now that you have read this book, you know what you are hearing and seeing—and, above all, *doing*—at Mass. All that remains is to participate with a fresh understanding and let Eucharist become the "source and summit of your Christian life." And share it with others.

May "the grace of our Lord Jesus Christ, and the love of the Father, and the communion of the Holy Spirit be with you!"
Amen.

For prayer and discussion:

- How has this last chapter given you a "road map" or "spiritual growth plan" for growing to the fullness of the Christian life?

- Which of the five steps ("starting points") have you consciously taken? Which of the five "phases" of spiritual growth best describes your life as you experience it right now?

- How does the Eucharist remind you of each daily starting point and support you in it?

- Do you see how, in Eucharist, you can experience the progress made from each starting point and draw encouragement from it?

- Do you want to learn more about this path to perfection? (If so, go to *www.immersedinchrist.com*.)